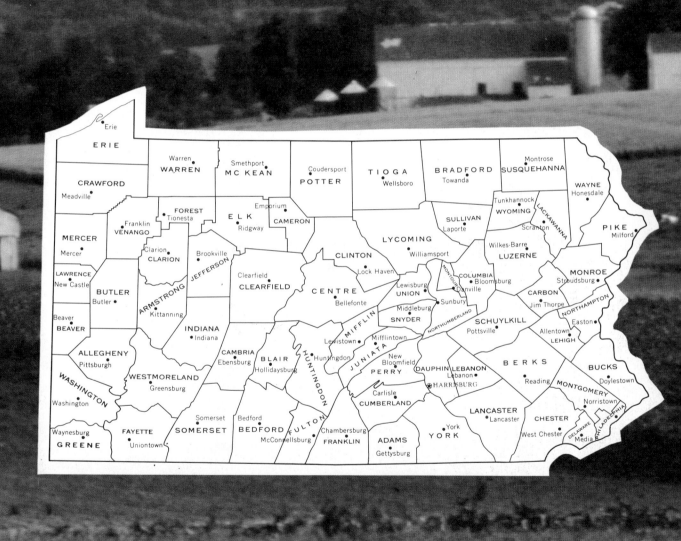

The New

Enchantment of America

PENNSYLVANIA

By Allan Carpenter

 CHILDRENS PRESS, CHICAGO

ACKNOWLEDGMENTS

For assistance in the preparation of the revised edition, the author thanks:
JOYCE M. ISBICKI, Photo Librarian, Bureau of Travel Development, Department of Commerce, Commonwealth of Pennsylvania.

American Airlines—Anne Vitaliano, Director of Public Relations; *Capitol Historical Society,* Washington, D. C.; *Newberry Library,* Chicago, Dr. Lawrence Towner, Director; *Northwestern University Library,* Evanston, Illinois; *United Airlines*—John P. Grember, Manager of Special Promotions; Joseph P. Hopkins, Manager, News Bureau.

UNITED STATES GOVERNMENT AGENCIES: *Department of Agriculture*—Robert Hailstock, Jr., Photography Division, Office of Communication; Donald C. Schuhart, Information Division, Soil Conservation Service. *Army*—Doran Topolosky, Public Affairs Office, Chief of Engineers, Corps of Engineers. *Department of Interior*—Louis Churchville, Director of Communications; EROS Space Program—Phillis Wiepking, Community Affairs; Charles Withington, Geologist; Mrs. Ruth Herbert, Information Specialist; Bureau of Reclamation; National Park Service—Fred Bell and the individual sites; Fish and Wildlife Service—Bob Hines, Public Affairs Office. *Library of Congress*—Dr. Alan Fern, Director of the Department of Research; Sara Wallace, Director of Publications; Dr. Walter W. Ristow, Chief, Geography and Map Division; Herbert Sandborn, Exhibits Officer. *National Archives*—Dr. James B. Rhoads, Archivist of the United States; Albert Meisel, Assistant Archivist for Educational Programs; David Eggenberger, Publications Director; Bill Leary, Still Picture Reference; James Moore, Audio-Visual Archives. *United States Postal Service*—Herb Harris, Stamps Division.

For assistance in the preparation of the first edition, the author thanks:
Dr. S.K. Stevens, Executive Director, Pennsylvania Historical and Museum Commission; William W. Scranton, Governor; Neal V. Musmanno, Deputy Superintendent, Department of Public Instruction, Commonwealth of Pennsylvania; Genevieve Blatt, Secretary of Internal Affairs, Commonwealth of Pennsylvania; Robert R. Shoemaker, Director Travel Development Bureau, Department of Commerce, Commonwealth of Pennsylvania; Kenneth V. Gardner, Wildlife Education Specialist, Pennsylvania Game Commission; R.N. Williams, II, Director, The Historical Society of Pennsylvania; Department of Forests and Waters, Commonwealth of Pennsylvania; Department of Agriculture, Commonwealth of Pennsylvania.

Illustrations on the preceding pages:
Cover photograph: Hopewell Village, nineteenth century ironmaking community, USDI, NPS, Hopewell Village National Historic Site
Page 1: Commemorative stamps of historic interest
Pages 2-3: Amish Farm, Bureau of Travel Development, Pennsylvania Department of Commerce
Page 3 (Map): USDI Geological Survey
Pages 4-5: Philadelphia area, EROS Space Photo, USDI Geological Survey, EROS Data Center

Project Editor, Revised Edition:
 Joan Downing
Assistant Editor, Revised Edition:
 Mary Reidy

Library of Congress Cataloging in Publication Data

Carpenter, John Allan, 1917-
 Pennsylvania.

 (The New Enchantment of America)
 SUMMARY: Introduces the Keystone State, its history from the earliest time to the present, its famous citizens, and places of interest.
 1. Pennsylvania—Juvenile literature. [1. Pennsylvania] I. Title
 F149.3.C3 1978 974.8 78-5089
 ISBN 0-516-04138-X

Contents

A True Story to Set the Scene

"I dreamed that Tarachawagon gave Shikellamy a fine rifle." As he said the words, the old chief, Shikellamy, looked with pleasure on the beautiful rifle owned by Conrad Weiser, the Pennsylvania Indian agent who was called Tarachawagon by the Indians. There was an ancient Indian custom that whenever someone had a dream about a gift, the owner was obliged to make the dream come true. So the rifle changed hands.

Not long afterward, Weiser again met the aged chief; smiling, Weiser said: "I dreamed that Shikellamy presented me with the large and beautiful island situated in the Susquehanna River." As Shikellamy later gave over the deed to the valuable property, he looked rather regretfully at the Indian agent and remarked, "Tarachawagon, let us never dream again." This property is now the Island of Que, in the river opposite Selinsgrove.

The life story of Chief Shikellamy, a man of "remarkable kindness, dignity, sobriety and prudence," reminds us of the long procession of leaders, statesmen, diplomats, scholars, and warriors of many races and countries whose unique contributions have enhanced the enchantment of Pennsylvania.

The name Shikellamy means "Our Enlightener." He claimed to be a Cayuga, captured and adopted by the Oneida. In 1728 he became the ambassador to Pennsylvania of the great Iroquois confederacy, the Six Nations. His headquarters village (called Shamokin) was at the forks of the Susquehanna, where Sunbury now stands.

Shikellamy conducted much important business between the government of Pennsylvania and the Iroquois council at Onandaga, New York. He attended most of the councils held at Philadelphia, Conestoga, and elsewhere and was responsible for the arrangements and outcome of many of these. Weiser considered him the key member of the Iroquois.

Opposite: The Island of Que today, looking north. The Susquehanna River is on the right.

9

The old chief was much concerned with the welfare of the Indian people. When the prohibition against selling liquor to the Indians ceased to be enforced, Shikellamy warned that unless matters were corrected friendly relations between the government and the Six Nations would cease. Improvements were quickly brought about.

Shikellamy persuaded the colonial government to establish a forge at Shamokin so that the Indians' rifles and other metal implements could be repaired. In return, Shikellamy permitted a Moravian mission to operate at Shamokin. The chief helped missionary David Zeisberger to prepare an Onandaga dictionary.

Missionary Count Nicholas Ludwig Von Zinzendorf presented the chief with a silver knife, fork, and spoon and an ivory drinking cup richly mounted in silver. With this was given a message urging the chief to hold fast to the gospel which he had heard from the count's own lips. Shortly afterward, Shikellamy became a Christian.

On his way to Shamokin, Shikellamy became so ill he barely had the strength to reach home. Zeisberger cared for the stricken chief until Shikellamy's death on December 6, 1748. The colonial government sent a message of condolence and many fine presents to the family.

Shikellamy, with Weiser's help, had maintained friendly relations between the English and the Iroquois. Pennsylvania escaped a Six-Nation war. A French alliance with the Iroquois would have threatened the destruction of all the English colonies on the coast.

Another great Iroquois leader, Cornplanter, *by F. Bartoli.*

Lay of the Land

"What resources an industrious, ambitious and conscientious man can find here! An abundance of food, of low-priced land, of rich, unworked soil . . . magnificent cloak of forest. . . . These rare and precious advantages are bound to provide human growth with all the vigor and richness it can assimilate. Who knows how far all this progress can expand in a half century?"

A journey through the wonderful land of Pennsylvania in the 1750s inspired this remarkable description and prophecy by the French traveler, Michel-Guillaume de Crèvecoeur.

THE LAND TODAY

This land that impressed the wise Frenchman so many years ago is greatly varied. The variety is shown by the fact that Pennsylvania is the only state with direct water access to the Atlantic Ocean, the Great Lakes, and the Ohio-Mississippi river system.

Pennsylvania's boundaries follow natural lines only in the forty-mile (sixty-four-kilometer) stretch on Lake Erie and the portions touched by the Delaware River. Pennsylvania is bounded by six states: New York, Ohio, West Virginia, Maryland, Delaware, and New Jersey.

Mountains and valleys cut diagonally across Pennsylvania from northeast to southwest. The state has several distinct geographic areas: a small strip of coastal plain; the Piedmont district; the Blue Ridge; the New England upland; the Great Valley; the Appalachian Mountain section; the great Allegheny Plateau, which covers almost half of the commonwealth; and a small strip of glacial lowland along the shore of Lake Erie.

Seven ridges of the Appalachian Mountains furrow the land. The mountains of Pennsylvania include the Blue Ridge, the Poconos, and the Alleghenies.

A broad belt of wide valleys alternates with the narrow mountain ridges. Divisions of the Great Valley are called the Cumberland,

11

The deep cleft of the Delaware Water Gap was carved by river forces.

Lehigh, and Lebanon valleys. Other clefts in the land have been carved by river forces, such as the great southeastern 1,200-foot-deep (365.76 kilometers) gash of the Delaware Water Gap and the northern gorge cut through the rock by Pine Creek. This is known as the Grand Canyon of Pennsylvania.

Pennsylvania claims more rivers and streams than any other state. Three great river systems drain Pennsylvania: the Delaware, the Susquehanna, and the Ohio. The largest area of the commonwealth (20,917 square miles/54,174.82 square kilometers) is drained by the Susquehanna, the river called "The Tree of Peace" by the Indians. The Sinnemahoning, Juniata, and the West Branch of the Susquehanna are major parts of the Susquehanna system.

At Pittsburgh, where the Monongahela and Allegheny rivers form a Y, the tail of that Y becomes the mighty Ohio River. The Allegheny flows through Pennsylvania for 300 miles (482.8 kilometers) and the Monongahela for 91 miles (146.45 kilometers). Other tributaries of the Ohio system are the Youghioheny, Beaver and Clarion. The Schuylkill and Lehigh rivers flow into the Delaware.

Kinzua Reservoir, formed by the Allegheny Dam nine miles (14.48 kilometers) above Warren, is the largest man-made lake in the East. The 1,915-foot-long (583.69 meters) dam forms a curiously shaped body of water that extends far up into New York State, with another arm stretching along almost half the length of Kinzua Creek. Dams form many man-made lakes in Pennsylvania, including Lake Pymatuning. In the Indian language this name means "crooked-mouthed man's dwelling place." Lake Wallenpaupak is the largest lake entirely within Pennsylvania. Conneaut Lake, west of Meadville, is the largest natural body of water in Pennsylvania.

IN ANCIENT TIMES

The changes that have taken place in the land now called Pennsylvania during the past hundreds of millions of years are sometimes unknown and often almost impossible to comprehend. Ancient seas covered the land many times. Exactly how many times parts of Pennsylvania were beneath the sea as the land rose and fell will never be known.

About two hundred million years ago, unbelievable pressure from beneath the earth's surface folded the tremendous layer of surface

The Grand Canyon of Pennsylvania in Tiogo County (left) was cut through the rock by Pine Creek.

rocks into a jumble of mountains, some of them miles high. Over eons of time these great mountains were worn flat by wind and water. Then the earth began to rise again, and the ancient mountain tops were once more pushed upward. As streams flowed more swiftly, the waters cut soil away from the rocks, forming some valleys and filling others with hundreds of feet of earth.

Much later, great glaciers grew in the north and pushed down into what is now the United States. These glaciers came and melted four separate times. But only the last two came into what is now called Pennsylvania. The first of these was the glacier known as Illinoisan. It covered the northeastern and northwestern corners of what is now the commonwealth. Later the Wisconsin glacier moved into the same areas but did not reach quite as far. Big Pocono Mountain may have been the only land left standing above those portions of Pennsylvania that were buried by the last glacier.

These glaciers filled in some valleys and carved others more deeply. They pushed in and left rich soils as well as tons of boulders, sand, and gravel.

Comparatively few remains of ancient animals have been found in Pennsylvania. The oldest of these are simple worms; later came primitive types of shell fish and crustaceans. Dinosaurs and much later forms such as birds and mammals—even including the wooly mammoth and the southern peccary—have all left their traces on this land.

CLIMATE

Although Pennsylvania is near the ocean, it has a "continental" climate because its prevailing winds bring the weather of the heart of the continent to it, for the most part. There are extremes of heat and cold, but not so marked as in the central states. Southeastern Pennsylvania and the Lake Erie region have the longest frost-free periods. The higher lands have three to five months free from frost. Rain and snow falls total just under forty inches (101.6 centimeters) in the yearly average.

Footsteps on the Land

Pennsylvania occupies a unique and honored place in American history. It was the birthplace of the Declaration of Independence, the Constitution of the United States, and the Gettysburg Address. Many claim for it the title "Birth-State of the Nation."

The union was conceived and framed at Philadelphia and preserved in the quiet Pennsylvania college town of Gettysburg. The background of all these and many other events is stirring and interesting.

BEFORE THE RECORDS BEGAN

Little is known about people who occupied what is now Pennsylvania before Europeans first came to the region. At Sheep Rock near Huntingdon, archaeologists have discovered the bones of human beings who lived in the region at least six thousand years ago. Probably there were people in the area centuries before that.

AN ABORIGINAL DWELLING PLACE

The lone Indian brave sang on and on. He called on each of the animal spirits by name and invited them to attend the feast. A chorus of Indian women accompanied him, first with their voices, then with dancing. The roasted head of a bear was passed around on a skewer so that each member of the tribe could take a bite. Study of such works as this "Dark Dance" help us to understand the centuries-old culture of the people who were found when the first Europeans came into what is now Pennsylvania.

Then the most important group in the region called themselves the Lennai Lenape; they came to be known by Europeans as the Delaware.

The Delaware were dominated by the fierce and powerful Iroquois Confederacy, a group of "Five Nations," which later became the

"Six Nations." Guns the Iroquois had obtained from early Dutch settlers of New York helped them to overcome almost all opposition of other Indian tribes, making them subject to Iroquois rule. At regular intervals, the Delaware carried large amounts of wampum as a tribute they were forced to pay their "uncles," the Iroquois.

Only one Iroquois Confederacy tribe, the Seneca, occupied much of what is now Pennsylvania, but some other non-federated Iroquois tribes also lived there.

The Huron Indians were almost destroyed by the Confederacy. Another powerful language-related Iroquois tribe was the Susquehannock, not a part of the Confederacy. They first beat back an attack by the warriors of the Iroquois Confederacy, but eventually most of them were killed or driven out of the area.

The remnants were known as the Conestoga Indians. This once-haughty group was finally massacred by a renegade band of Europeans known as the Paxton Boys, and the last one was killed.

Members of the Shawnee group also played an important part in Pennsylvania.

Indian women carried on the gardening, and the men did the hunting. Indian authority John Witthoft has said, "The Indian woman was no drudge but a matriarch who owned her own house and fields, controlled the food supplies of the household and held greater authority than any man within the family and community. . . . She held an elevated position. . . ."

Deer was the most important game for Indian hunters in the region, and an Indian brave could walk for miles carrying a whole deer carcass on his back. The bear was much respected and admired, and many Indians considered the bear to be something like a man in a hairy skin. There were many legends of lost men who went to live with the bears or of lost children who were adopted by bear families.

Indians saw themselves as a part of Nature. They did not think that they had any power to control the world about them, and they felt they survived only because they kept their place in Nature's plan. They considered that the land and the resources of the land were to be used by all, and they would have been horrified to think that the land could "belong" to any one group or individual.

When European people began to come into the Indians' lands, their ideas and manner of life were so different that it was almost impossible for the two groups to understand one another. This was one of the reasons for the almost two centuries of trouble between Indians and Europeans, much of which was avoided in Pennsylvania because of the care taken by the founders to do justice to the Indians.

A BIG TUB AND A LITTLE SETTLEMENT

Pennsylvania was probably visited by Europeans long before we have any record of this event. Traders, fishermen, and others very likely reached the region at an early date. By the time known Europeans first reached Pennsylvania, they found that the Indians had many belongings that had been made by Europeans. Some feel that Spaniards built a fort in the 1500s on what is now called Spanish Hill near Waverly. The Indians had a legend about this, and a Spanish sword, crucifix, and medal have all been found in the neighborhood. However, Spanish occupation is considered "highly legendary."

The famous Captain John Smith of Virginia might be listed as the "discoverer" of Pennsylvania. In 1608, only a year after Jamestown, Virginia, was founded, Captain Smith came overland and went up the Susquehanna. Some authorities say that he did not get quite as far north as present-day Pennsylvania, while others say that honor goes to him.

Henry Hudson, employed by the Dutch, sailed up a great bay in 1609 and gave the Dutch a claim to the region. In 1610, Captain Samuel Argall of Virginia named this bay in honor of Lord de la Warr, governor of Virginia, and it became Delaware Bay. The most complete early exploration was that of Etienne Brulé, who traveled the Susquehanna from its source to its mouth in 1615-1616, four years before the Pilgrims landed at Plymouth.

Sweden became interested in obtaining American power and trade and sent several expeditions. One of these came in 1643 under the leadership of a most unusual man, Johan Printz, who weighed 400 pounds (181.4 kilograms) and was called "Big Tub" by the Indians.

At Tinicum Island he established the first permanent settlement in what is now Pennsylvania.

This Swedish settlement provided the first church (Lutheran), the first school, and the first court in what today is Pennsylvania.

The Dutch established a trading post in present-day Pennsylvania in 1647. Then in 1655 the Swedish colonies in the area were seized by the Dutch on the command of the Dutch governor at New York, famed Peter Stuyvesant. The Dutch ruled for nine years, until in 1664 the colonies of the Delaware River region were seized by the English in the name of the Duke of York.

WILLIAM PENN'S HOLY EXPERIMENT

King Charles II of England owed William Penn 16,000 pounds for a loan from Penn's late father. When Penn requested that the loan be repaid by a grant of land in America instead of cash, the king granted this favor because of his friendship for the senior Penn. On March 4, 1681, King Charles granted to Penn by royal charter a territory larger than that ever controlled by any other one Englishman aside from the kings—more than 28,000,000 acres (11,331,208 hectares). This huge tract stretched from the Delaware River on the east across five whole degrees of longitude to the west. It reached from the 39th degree of latitude on the south to the 42nd on the north. Penn's grant was almost as large as all of England. The next year Penn's friend the Duke of York deeded to Penn an additional tract, including what is now the state of Delaware. For this enormous "kingdom" Penn was required to pay to the king two beaver skins each year to symbolize his allegiance to the Crown.

Modest William Penn wanted to call his province either New Wales or Sylvania, but the king insisted on giving it "a name." As Penn himself wrote, "the King would give it in honor of my father . . . whom he often mentions with praise." That name, of course, was Pennsilvania—Penn's woods. That was the original spelling.

Penn's cousin William Markham was sent to America as deputy governor in April, 1681, to take possession of the colony and to "lay out a great towne." Penn remained in England to create a government for the new colony, and attend to other details. In October, 1682, William Penn arrived in America on board the ship *Welcome*.

"The air is sweet and clear, the Heavens serene," Penn wrote. "The country itself . . . is not to be despised . . . in some places a vast fat earth, like our best vales, in England . . . God, in his wisdom, having ordered it so that the advantages of the country are divided; the back lands being generally three-to-one richer than those that lie by navigable rivers."

Almost all of Penn's grant was covered by great, primeval forests, stretching west as far as man could see from the highest peak. Some trees measured 14 feet (4.27 meters) at the base and towered 200 feet (60.96 meters). Here and there were marshes and a few open fields, burned by the Indians to round up buffalo, elk, or black bear.

By the time Penn arrived there were perhaps five hundred scattered Dutch, Swedish, and other settlers in what is now Pennsylvania. Philadelphia, Penn's "great towne," had already been started as the capital of the country. Eighty houses were built there in the first year. A distinguished group of settlers was attracted by Penn's policies of freedom and by the promotion and advertising that Penn had done in England.

The first General Assembly of the colony, held at Chester on December 4, adopted the "Great Law," drawn up by William Penn on the basis of his beliefs as a Quaker. No man was to have life, liberty, or property taken away except by trial before a jury of twelve. Voting was granted to all males who believed in God and met moderate property requirements. The death penalty applied only to treason and murder. Children were to be instructed in reading, writing, and "some useful trade or skill."

Today those rights may seem modest, but in those times when rights for the common man were almost unknown, these liberal laws were hailed as Penn's "Holy Experiment." An experiment, as one writer put it, "that might well be termed the wellspring of democracy."

In this and in revisions of the government in 1683 and 1701, William Penn signed away for the good of others what might have

Benjamin West's famous 1771 painting of William Penn trading on a friendly basis with the Indians.

been his almost complete personal power, so that as he said "the will of one man may not hinder the good of an whole country." He left himself "no power of doing mischief."

William Penn considered the Indians to be his good neighbors. Although he was not legally required to reach any agreement with them for the use of the land, one of his first acts was to sign his famous treaty with the Indians for the purchase of their lands. This was not the first treaty with the Indians, but it was one of the most fair.

Historian John F. Watson wrote that Penn's "first care was to promote peace with all . . . and strictly enjoined the inhabitants and surveyors not to settle any land to which the Indians had a claim until he had first, at his own cost, satisfied and paid them for the same. . . . Which discreet method so effectually engaged their friendship that they entirely loved him and his people—when at the same time several of the neighboring colonies were at war and in great distress by the Indians."

20

For his first Pennsylvania purchase, William Penn paid the Indians 350 fathoms of wampum, 300 gilders, 20 white blankets, 20 kettles, 20 guns, 20 coats, 50 shirts, pipes, scissors, shoes, combs, hoes, tobacco, knives, and other merchandise.

The French philosopher Voltaire called Penn's Indian agreements "the only treaty never sworn to and never broken." And so began a period of seventy years of friendship with the Indians. Even in later years of Indian warfare it was said that no Quaker was knowingly killed by the Indians.

In 1684 Penn felt he must return to England. During the two years spent in America he had organized the province of Pennsylvania with probably the most just laws in the world of the time. He "set up courts and magistrates; laid out Philadelphia; established friendly relations with the Dutch and Swedish colonists, and with the Indians; and had visited New York, Western New Jersey and Maryland."

During his stay in England, William Penn suffered many discouragements. He was accused of conspiracy against the King of England, and the right to govern Pennsylvania was taken away from him in 1692. He was acquitted of the charge of treason by King William, and Pennsylvania was restored to him in 1694. He returned to America with his second wife, Hannah, in 1699. Shortly after they arrived, Penn's son John was born—the first child of his second marriage and his first child to be born in America.

In 1701 Penn granted his last and most democratic frame of government. It was called a Charter of Privileges, said to be one of the most advanced democratic governments of the time, and has been called the "most famous of all colonial constitutions, because it contained many of the most important features of all workable written constitutions."

At that time, also, the three lower counties, which later became the state of Delaware, were given the right to separate from Pennsylvania.

After a stay of only two years in America, in 1701 Penn again returned to England. The Delaware Indians gathered from great distances to bid him farewell. He never saw his beloved American colony again and died in England in 1718. His second wife, Hannah, and his sons, John, Thomas, and Richard Penn, took part in the management of Pennsylvania affairs, but in 1776 the Penn family lost control of the colony. However, the contributions made by William Penn have continued to influence the commonwealth throughout the years.

A WALK EVEN TO DEATH

One of William Penn's early purchases of land from the Indians included land as far north as a man could walk in three days. Penn took only half of this "walk" at the time. When European settlement began to go beyond these boundaries, Penn's sons, in 1737 as the proprietors of Pennsylvania, called for the other half of the treaty to be put into effect—to include all the land in another day and a half of walking. The Indians thought this would be only about forty miles (sixty-four kilometers) from the starting point. However, the proprietors had selected three strong runners and promised five hundred acres (more than two hundred hectares) of land and five pounds to the one who would cover the greatest distance within the time.

Edward Marshall, Solomon Jennings, and James Yeates started from a chestnut tree at the present site of Wrightstown; increasing their pace, they were soon virtually running, much to the dismay of the Indians, who had expected a leisurely walk. Fatigue forced Jennings to quit; he never regained his health and died a few years later; Yeates collapsed and died from overexertion within two or three days; Marshall reached more than sixty miles (ninety-six kilometers) from the starting point without damage to his health, and he lived to be ninety.

The Indians felt they had been cheated in this infamous "Walking Purchase"; they never forgot this loss of faith, and from that time onward, relations with the Indians continued to grow worse. This was about ten years after Chief Shikellamy became the ambassador to Pennsylvania of the great Iroquois confederacy.

WAR WITH THE FRENCH AND INDIANS

French traders were active in western Pennsylvania by the 1740s. In 1749, Celeron de Bienville explored the area and buried the famous lead plates laying claim to it for the King of France as part of the vast western empire they hoped to rule in North America. Until the 1750s, however, the French had not fortified or occupied that Pennsylvania land. In 1750 they established a trading post at the important Indian village of Chininqué (Logstown), headquarters for the Iroquois, Shawnee, and Delaware of the region and a great trading center of the Ohio Valley. This was about eighteen miles (about twenty-nine kilometers) south of present Pittsburgh.

By this time Pennsylvania had become "the most advanced of all the American colonies," according to Swiss historian Acrelius. It was clear to the French that before long the British would push their claim to western Pennsylvania.

In 1753 the French sent troops from Canada to strengthen their claims. They built Fort Presque Isle, at present-day Erie, and then with tremendous difficulty, brought men and supplies inland to build Fort Le Boeuf at present-day Waterford.

This fort played an interesting part in American history because to it in 1753 came one of the country's future leaders. At the age of twenty-one he was on his first mission for his country. Governor Dinwiddie of Virginia, which then also claimed this part of Pennsylvania, chose the youthful George Washington to take a message to the French commander demanding that they abandon their fort. He was guided by famed frontiersman Christopher Gist and several Indians. Travel through what he described as "excessive rains, snows and bad traveling through many mires and swamps" was difficult. Finally, however, Washington, even at that age called a "person of distinction" by the Virginia governor, delivered his message. The reply he received indicated that the French intended to stay and defend themselves if necessary.

After a fatiguing return journey, in which he was also shot at by Indians and nearly drowned crossing the icy Allegheny River, Washington brought back the message and his complete journal. The journal was published and attracted favorable attention to the young man who had proved to be such a keen observer.

By the time Washington returned, a Virginia force was already at work building a fort where the Allegheny and Monongahela join to make the Ohio River. Before this was finished, it was captured by the French. The French built their own fort there and called it Fort Duquesne.

Washington by now had returned to western Pennsylvania with a force under the command of Colonel Joshua Fry. When Fry died of an injury, Washington was next in command. He started to build a fort, southeast of present-day Uniontown, which he called Necessity, because of the desperate situation.

When an Indian ally, Half King, brought word that a French force was hidden close by, Washington and his men with Half King and his men marched through a rainy night to attack the French on the morning of May 28, 1754. The French leader, Coulon de Jumonville, and several of his men were killed. All but one of the rest were captured. This little engagement on the slope of Laurel Mountain in what is now Fayette County was the first battle of the French and Indian War.

As British leader Robert Walpole said, "The volley fired by a young Virginian (Washington) in the backwoods of America, set the world on fire."

The French quickly pushed forward a force much stronger than Washington's, attacked Fort Necessity before it was finished, and forced Washington to surrender on July 3, 1754—the first and only time in his whole career that he surrendered.

Washington wrote: "When the French called to parley . . . about midnight we agreed that each side should retire without molestation . . . that we should march away with all the honours of war and with all our stores, effects and baggage."

In 1755 the British sent General Edward Braddock, commander of all British troops in North America, with an army of 1,450 British regulars to cut a path through the wilderness. A smaller French and Indian force marched out in some fear from Fort Duquesne to meet him. The British regulars were ambushed. Hidden behind the trees,

24

The defeat of General Braddock, from an old lithograph.

the French and their Indian allies could easily pick them off one by one. Braddock was injured and George Washington was left in command, trying to form a rear guard. When General Braddock died, young Washington is said to have read the funeral service in the heart of the lonely woods. However, authorities feel there probably was no time for this.

This major defeat left much of Pennsylvania almost completely in the hands of the French and their Indian allies. "Indian war parties were sent out by the French to ravage the frontiers of Pennsylvania and other colonies. The war cry and tomahawk brought fear and death into the peaceful province of Pennsylvania which had not been touched by any of the earlier colonial wars."

Beginning in 1756, Fort Augusta was built, the first of a chain of British outposts in the wilderness. By 1758 General John Forbes was able to bring an enormous army of seventy-five hundred soldiers and one thousand helpers into the wilderness. They built and marched from Carlisle by way of Bedford over what has come to be called Forbes' Road. He took Fort Duquesne which the French had blown up and deserted, ending that part of the war which took place in Pennsylvania. Forbes ordered the fort rebuilt and named Fort Pitt; he named the place "Pittsburgh."

Warfare was not over, however, because the Indians again went on the warpath under the leadership of Chief Pontiac. When the forces of Pontiac laid siege to Fort Pitt in 1763, Colonel Henry Bouquet was sent with five hundred troops to relieve the fort. Before he reached it, the Indians attacked him. Bouquet made a barricade from sacks of flour his party was carrying, and in the battle of the "Flour-bag Fort," near Jeannette, Bouquet raised the siege of Fort Pitt and broke the back of the Pontiac conspiracy in the area.

ONE FROM MANY

With the western lands at last in some peace and safety, a start toward the settlement of western Pennsylvania was possible. Large numbers of settlers of many nationalities and religious backgrounds were rapidly filling the eastern lands. The settlers who came to Pennsylvania in ever-increasing numbers gave it the most mixed population of all the early American colonies.

Religion was an important element in early Pennsylvania. The Quakers saw in Pennsylvania their chance to establish a government in accord with their religion, giving them relief from persecution because of their beliefs, and better commercial conditions.

The two great religious philosophies of the colonies were those of the New England Puritans and Pilgrims and the Quakers. As someone has said, "The Puritan concept lost; the Quaker concept won." Where the "Puritans were intolerant, the Quakers were tolerant, and toleration has triumphed."

Quaker concern for others is shown by the fact that over the years Pennsylvania Quakers have organized thirty-five large organizations of social concern, many of them worldwide in scope, providing help to the poor, the oppressed, and all who need aid of many kinds.

The first Catholic congregation was organized at Philadelphia in 1720. In the 1740s Henry M. Muhlenberg helped the Lutherans to begin a growth that has made them the largest Protestant denomination in Pennsylvania today. The first Presbyterian church in Pennsylvania was organized in 1698. At a later date both the Evangelical and

26

United Brethren churches were created in Pennsylvania. The first Jewish congregation in Pennsylvania was organized in 1776.

Scots and Scotch-Irish, French Huguenots, Irish, and Welsh all came to join the Swedish, Dutch, and English who first arrived in Pennsylvania. Probably the outstanding nationality in Pennsylvania has been German *(Deutsch)*. These people came to be known as the "Pennsylvania Dutch."

Attracted by freedom from wars and oppression and by the opportunity to succeed by farming, large numbers of German people came to the colony that had been founded by a man who loved and understood the oppressed. The first record of Germans in America concerns the ship *Concord,* which arrived at Philadelphia in 1683 with thirteen families. They reached this land of promise and freedom after a difficult sea voyage. In those days most sea voyages were difficult and food was scarce. Many later immigrants had to agree to become indentured servants for two to seven years to pay their expenses.

The Pennsylvania Germans belong to many groups and sects, including the Mennonites, Amish, German Baptist Brethren or Dunkers, Schwenkfelders, and Moravians. Some of these (Mennonites, Amish, Dunkers, and River Brethren) are known as the "Plain People." Even today, the Plain People wear characteristic dress. The men wear great, broad-brimmed, black felt hats, full beards with no mustaches, bright blue work shirts, and suspendered black trousers. The women wear black bonnets and homemade, ankle-length dresses of one of the permitted colors—blue, purple, rose, or green.

"All things about these people—their clothing, their hair styles, why the men never wear belts, how their homes are decorated, their language—their whole lives from birth in the kitchen to death in a fitted handmade coffin—all are governed by religious traditions far removed from the mainstream of modern American living." About 10 percent of the Pennsylvania Dutch are the Plain People.

Lead by Count Zinzendorf, the Moravians came to Pennsylvania in 1741. They founded the town of Bethlehem, which was named by the count on a Christmas Eve as he listened to Christmas carols.

"This colony became one of the most cultured in America. Hayden's and Mozart's symphonies and string quartets were played in Bethlehem before they were ever heard in Boston or Philadelphia. The Moravian service at Bethlehem on Christmas Eve dates back to 1752. It is a musical joy. On Easter Sunday the famed trombone choir calls the church members to the graveyard to greet the Easter sunrise." Altogether the German people in Pennsylvania have brought a rich heritage to America.

They have given us Santa Claus, the Christmas tree, the Easter rabbit, and the classical American barn design, among other things. Their reputation for good cooking is known around the world, and their recipes are much in demand. Their painted designs, furniture, and other craftwork place them high in the ranks of craft culture. They brought customs of piety, thrift, responsibility, industry, and good humor which rank among the best traditions of the country.

Most of the Pennsylvania Dutch live in Lancaster County (below), which is often referred to as "Amish Country."

CRADLE OF LIBERTY

As Pennsylvania and the other colonies grew and prospered, the control of the British king and his government became more distasteful to many. Pennsylvania, with its traditions of local rule and individual freedom and with Philadelphia as the largest city of the colonies and a leading cultural center, quite naturally became a leader in the movement to resist the king's many taxes and other unpopular acts.

The growing spirit of revolt was shown at Fort Louden as early as 1765. Settlers of that region objected to British attempts to reopen trade with the Indians. A young settler, James Smith, led a group disguised as Indians who burned "King's Goods" carried in a pack train. Eight of Smith's "Indians" were captured and imprisoned in the fort. Smith captured enough British soldiers so that the British had to give up their captives in exchange. Then Smith led three hundred settlers to the fort; the troops there were eventually forced to withdraw.

In 1769 James Smith and eighteen volunteers surprised and overcame the defenders of Fort Bedford to set free some settlers who had been made prisoner there for defying British regulations. Smith later wrote: "This was the first British fort in America that was taken by what they called 'American rebels.'" Although the Revolution did not begin for several years, in a sense this might be considered true. Such resistance to oppression grew and spread as the years passed.

When the First Continental Congress met at Carpenters' Hall in Philadelphia in 1774, the city became, in effect, the first national capital. The Pennsylvania assembly was the first of all the colonies to ratify the work of the first Congress. The Second Continental Congress began its work at the State House (later Independence Hall) in 1775. This Congress selected George Washington as commander-in-chief of a war that had already begun in Massachusetts—the Revolutionary War. It was this Congress that made Philadelphia the site of what is probably the most noted single event in American history—the signing of the Declaration of Independence on the first Fourth of

July in 1776. The declaration was first read publicly in Philadelphia. John Adams wrote, "The bells rang all day and almost all night."

There is a strange story that at the very moment the distinguished Congress was meeting in Philadelphia, a group of settlers at Pine Creek met under the "Tiadaghton Elm" on July 4, 1776, and declared their independence from England, without knowing that the Congress was doing the same thing.

In that same year, under the leadership of Benjamin Franklin, Pennsylvania created a new state constitution, a document so liberal in its declaration of human rights that it was much copied by the other former colonies in setting up their governments. Some of its ideas were even taken up by leaders of the French Revolution.

As the British general, Sir William Howe, pushed Washington's untrained troops across New Jersey, the capture of Philadelphia was threatened. This was postponed by Washington's success at Trenton, New Jersey, and later at Princeton.

Invasion of Pennsylvania was not put off for long. In the spring of 1777, General Howe and Prussian General Knyphausen at last advanced once more on Philadelphia. With only twelve thousand poorly trained, inadequately supplied men against eighteen thousand British and Hessian forces, General Washington attempted to halt the enemy advance at Brandywine Creek near Chadds Ford.

The Battle of Brandywine, probably the lowest point of American fortunes in the Revolution, ended with the victorious British forcing Washington to withdraw to Chester. Lafayette, the French ally of the Americans, although wounded, helped to reorganize the retreating troops. Polish ally Count Pulaski's cavalry protected them from attack.

In the panic at Philadelphia that followed this defeat, American patriots began to leave the city, and the Continental Congress moved its headquarters. The national government operated at Lancaster for one day, and then was moved to York.

Howe continued to advance and surprised a force of Continental troops under General Anthony Wayne at Paoli. The battle here has been called a massacre because the British were so ruthless. Three hundred American troops died at Paoli.

The Battle of Germantown, *a painting by Howard Pyle, shows General Washington's forces attacking the British in October, 1777.*

On September 26, 1777, Lord Howe occupied Philadelphia, where he was welcomed by the American Tories, colonists who had remained loyal to Britain. With the hope of drawing the British forces from Philadelphia, General Washington attacked the enemy in October at Germantown in what might have become a victory. They were, however, prevented by dense fog from carrying out their plans. General Washington took up headquarters at Whitemarsh.

At the Philadelphia home of Lydia Darrah, the British made plans to march on Whitemarsh. Ms. Darrah managed to get a pass for a pretended errand, and hurried off to warn General Washington. As a result of the warning, the American forces were able to hold off British troops in the Battle of Whitemarsh and Lydia Darrah became an American heroine.

While the British were enjoying their luxurious stay in comfortable Philadelphia—with balls, dinner parties, and theatricals—Washington stationed his troops at Valley Forge, where hardship was the lot of all. The sufferings of the tattered and poorly fed army are familiar to everyone. Not so well known is the fact that Baron Von Steuben was able to weld the undisciplined troops at Valley Forge into a competent army. Washington's position at Valley Forge kept the iron furnaces and powder mills of the region from falling into British hands, and kept the British from overrunning interior Pennsylvania.

At York, the temporary capital, a group headed by General Thomas Conway plotted to remove General Washington and install General Horatio Gates in his place. The plot was foiled by Lafayette, who rose at a meeting and drank a toast: "I propose the health of the commander-in-chief at Valley Forge. Gentlemen, I give you General George Washington!" All joined in the toast and Washington continued in command.

Continental Army huts at Valley Forge.

Lafayette himself was almost captured while the British occupied Philadelphia. Sent on a reconnoitering expedition, Lafayette and his forces were trapped by the British. The British commander even invited a number of prominent people of Philadelphia to meet the marquis when he was in their hands. The British knew that Lafayette's capture would be a great blow to the Americans. At the last moment Lafayette discovered an avenue of escape and dashed away.

With the spring of 1778, the terrors of the winter at Valley Forge were left behind; British General Burgoyne suffered a great defeat in New York, and news came that Benjamin Franklin had been able to bring the French in on the American side. All of these events caused the British to release their hold on Philadelphia, and the Revolutionary battles moved from Pennsylvania to other areas.

During the war, the frontier Pennsylvania settlements suffered greatly as a result of British and Indian attacks. At Forty Fort, in Wyoming Valley, outnumbered colonists under Colonel Zebulon Butler and Nathan Denison were overcome in a battle with British and Indian forces. Although their terms of surrender called for the safety of the people, the Indians began a reign of terror, and three hundred men, women, and children were massacred.

Troops from Pennsylvania took part in almost every one of the war's campaigns. There were even many "Fighting Quakers" who felt more strongly for the Revolution than for their traditional hatred of war.

Pennsylvania contributed to the war effort in many ways. As the leading industrial region among the former colonies, Pennsylvania became the "Arsenal of the Revolution." The products of Pennsylvania's ironworks were so important that workers were forbidden to leave them, even for militia duty, without special permission. The Continental ordnance at Carlisle contributed a steady stream of muskets, cannon, swords, and other weapons. Even the Durham boats used by Washington in crossing the Delaware were a Pennsylvania invention. In 1775 Pennsylvania created its own navy as part of the defense of Pennsylvania, and this fleet fought several successful engagements.

By 1780 more than $6,000,000 had come to the Congress from Pennsylvania for the support of the war effort. Ninety Philadelphians helped further by subscribing a loan of about $1,500,000 to supply the army. Three famous Pennsylvanians did more than any others to finance the war effort: Benjamin Franklin through his efforts in France, and Robert Morris and Haym Salomon through their efforts in persuading others to loan money and even borrowing on their personal credit to supply Washington's army.

Many names of Pennsylvanians became famous for Revolutionary services, including those of Arthur St. Clair, Anthony Wayne, John Barry, John Armstrong, Thomas Mifflin, and Daniel Brodhead.

PENNSYLVANIA BECOMES A STATE

As a government for the new country, the Second Continental Congress, in 1777, had created at York the Articles of Confederation. The American nation tried to make this government work for eleven years, but it became plain that the Articles did not give the central government enough authority to carry on satisfactory work.

From May to September, 1787, a new convention met in Independence Hall, working on a new government. The efforts of several Pennsylvanians were critical in creating this new constitution. Without the counsel of Benjamin Franklin, it is doubtful if the job could have been done at all. Several times the aged leader kept the convention from breaking up entirely.

Pennsylvania's brilliant Gouverneur Morris was heard at the convention more frequently than any other man, and it has been said that the able Pennsylvania lawyer, James Wilson, was "the principal architect of the constitution, next to James Madison."

The new Constitution of the United States was finished at Philadelphia on September 17, 1787. The Pennsylvania Assembly was called, and ratified the new government on December 12. Pennsylvania became the second state of the United States, only five days behind Delaware, which not very long before had been a part of Pennsylvania.

*Left: Nicaragua salutes
the United States 200th
Birthday.*
Below: Scene at the
Signing of the Constitution
of the United States,
by Howard Chandler Christy.

Modern-day Pittsburgh (right) looks very different from the Pittsburgh of 1790 (below), as seen by an unknown artist.

Yesterday and Today

KEYSTONE IN A NEW COUNTRY

Pennsylvania itself adopted a new Commonwealth Constitution in 1790. In that year Philadelphia became the capital of the United States, retaining the seat of government until it was moved to Washington in 1800. In 1792 the federal government sold to Pennsylvania the region called the "Erie Triangle." This narrow wedge of land had been claimed by New York, Massachusetts, and Connecticut. Possession of this neck of land gave Pennsylvania its tremendously valuable outlet on the Great Lakes.

Philadelphia suffered a terrible epidemic of yellow fever in 1793. In that same year a strange event took place when refugees from the French Revolution bought land near present Towanda and built a settlement which they called Asylum because it gave them safety from the terrors of the French executions.

By the following spring, thirty rough houses had appeared at Asylum, located in Bradford County, northeast Pennsylvania. Although crude, many of the dwellings had chimneys, wallpaper, window glass, shutters, porches, and other touches of "elegance" to satisfy French tastes. Formerly wealthy and titled Frenchmen opened haberdashery shops, inns, and other businesses. They held elaborate costume parties in the wilderness.

A large log house (La Grande Maison) was built with the hope that Queen Marie Antoinette herself and her children could be rescued and brought to Asylum. It is interesting to think of the effect the coming of this grand lady might have had in frontier America. She was executed, however, and before long most of the colony drifted away.

Other new settlements lasted longer. Settlement was aided through the free "donation lands" paid to war veterans for their services in the Revolution. In 1783 the first trip westward was made by wagon to Pittsburgh. Up until this time such a feat had been considered impossible. One of the members of that wagon group described Pittsburgh as "sixty wooden houses and cabins in which live something more than one hundred families . . . the place reasonably expects to grow with the passage of time."

In the early 1790s another "war" came to the western Pennsylvania frontier. The settlers, protesting taxes on their strong drink, began the "Whiskey Rebellion." They held angry meetings, raised a militia, terrorized Pittsburgh, and forced revenue officers to flee for their lives. For a while matters seemed to be leading to a civil war, but Albert Gallatin persuaded many to give up the fight, and an army, authorized by Congress and dispatched by President Washington himself, suppressed the disturbance in Pennsylvania in 1794.

Another small and short-lived, but interesting, "rebellion" was the "Hot Water Rebellion" of 1798, centered in Quakertown. The federal government had laid a tax on various items, including land and houses. The house tax was assessed according to the number and size of windows. "The sight of assessors carefully measuring windows so irritated the Pennsylvania German housewives that they frequently greeted federal agents with a dash of hot water." Both the water and the tempers soon cooled, however.

In 1799 the government of Pennsylvania moved to a new capital—Lancaster. Thirteen years later, in 1812, the present capital, Harrisburg, became the seat of the government.

SECOND ROUND WITH ENGLAND

In that year the United States again went to war with England. One of the most interesting episodes of the War of 1812 took place in Pennsylvania. Most of the key forts in the west had fallen to Britain early in the war. American authorities realized that the western frontier would never be secure if British forces controlled the Great Lakes.

A Pennsylvanian, Captain Daniel Dobbins, was given the almost impossible task of building a strong naval fleet at Erie in the snug, protected harbor formed by Presque Isle Peninsula. Erie then was a tiny town of four hundred population. Pittsburgh had only six thousand people at the time. Skilled workers had to be brought from Philadelphia, and for much of the way there were no roads. Two hundred workers took five weeks to travel the 400 miles (643.7 kilometers) to Erie.

In spite of almost impossible difficulties, construction began, and work went on so quickly that at times trees that were growing in the morning had become planks nailed in ships by the time evening came—thanks to the genius of Dobbins, Noah Brown, his superintendent of construction, and Henry Eckford, designer.

At last the head of the growing fleet, Oliver Hazard Perry, arrived at Erie to take charge. One of those on the scene said, "The public never knew the worth of that man. They have known him only as the victor of the English fleet on Lake Erie, and yet this was far his smallest merit. Hundreds might have fought that battle as well as he did . . . But to appreciate his character, a person must have seen him, as I did, fitting out a fleet of six new vessels of war, . . . at some hundreds of miles from the sea coast . . . not one single article necessary for the equipment of a vessel . . . was not subject to land transportation of some 120 to 400 miles through roads nearly impassable. I have seen him, when almost abandoned by his country, with less than a hundred sailors under his command, and half of those on the sick list, toiling to fit out his fleet . . . evincing a courage far greater than what was required to fight the battle of the 10th of September."

The Battle of Lake Erie off Put-In Bay, *by William H. Powell, shows Oliver Hazard Perry's fleet taking the Great Lakes from British control.*

Preliminary work was begun in September, 1812. The bulk of the building of a complete fleet of ships was done in the incredibly short period of ninety days by men who had to begin the work by making their own tools from iron sheets and bars.

Perry won the Battle of Lake Erie, and the Great Lakes and western regions were taken from British control.

Stephen Girard of Philadelphia was especially helpful in arranging the country's finances during the War of 1812. Another leading Pennsylvanian in the war was famed Commodore Stephen Decatur. Pennsylvania's Albert Gallatin served as a peace commissioner in helping to work out the Treaty of Ghent, which closed the war and laid the foundations for an enduring peace.

GROWTH AND CHANGE

Under Governors J. Andrew Shulze and George Wolf great programs of canal building and other improvements were carried on. Social progress was shown in such developments as the Mechanics Union of Trade Associations formed at Philadelphia in 1827, the first of its kind in the United States. The Free School Act of 1834 provided a base for the growth of universal public education. A temporary set-back to Pennsylvania's advance came in the depression of 1837, but the rate of growth and progress was soon renewed.

The new Pennsylvania constitution of 1838 reduced the power of the governor, made more state positions elective, and gave the people "greater voice in government, protecting them from abuse of power."

One of the world's great scientific organizations had its beginnings in Philadelphia. The American Association of Geologists was formed there in 1840. It later became the powerful and respected American Association for the Advancement of Science.

During this period, in fact, Philadelphia was foremost in almost every field of science and culture. Its contributions were more national and less regional than those of New England. It led in the development of magazines, in music publishing, architecture, and, until 1830, in the theater. It had a dominant voice in literature, art, and music.

In this period, no other state even began to approach Pennsylvania's record in improved roads—with 3,000 miles (4,828 kilometers) of roads carrying people and goods across the commonwealth as early as 1832. Gas lighting came to Philadelphia in 1836, and the once-remote regions west of the Alleghenies were brought into instant touch with the world with the completion of the telegraph line in 1846. More Pennsylvania men enlisted for the Mexican War of 1846 than could be accepted for service.

OPPOSED TO OPPRESSION

Pennsylvania was one of the strongest and earliest leaders in the growing opposition to slavery. The first recorded protest against slavery in the United States was made by a group of Pennsylvania Germans as early as 1688. An anti-slavery society was formed at Philadelphia in 1775. In 1780 Pennsylvania passed an act gradually abolishing slavery in the commonwealth. The 1790 yearly meeting of the Quakers in Pennsylvania sent a protest to Congress on slavery. It is thought that the "Underground Railroad" for helping slaves to escape to Canada was given its name in Pennsylvania.

When Congress passed the Fugitive Slave Law, requiring runaway slaves to be returned to their masters from anywhere in the country, the first blood was shed in Pennsylvania in resisting this law. Edward Gorsuch came to Christiana from Maryland to recapture his slaves who had run away and hidden in the cabin of William Parker. Gorsuch declared that he would "get his property or breakfast in hell." Cries of "kidnapping" went up and many neighbors arrived. When Gorsuch started for the cabin, he was killed and his son shot. Parker and thirty-seven others were tried for treason, but Thaddeus Stevens, member of Congress from Lancaster, successfully defended them at their trial.

David Wilmot, of Bradford County, gained national fame when he introduced a motion in Congress to prohibit slavery in territory gained from Mexico after the war. The "Wilmot Proviso" was defeated in Congress, but it expressed the general feeling of the people of Pennsylvania.

Abraham Lincoln carried Pennsylvania in the election of 1860; this helped to put him in office. The February 11, 1860, edition of a Pennsylvania newspaper—the Chester County *Times* of West Chester—has the distinction of carrying what has been called the first published biography of Lincoln.

When Lincoln made his long, roundabout journey from Illinois on the way to his inauguration as president, he arrived in Harrisburg in time to hear that a plot to assassinate him had been uncovered. He was slipped on board a special train to Philadelphia; all telegraph lines from Harrisburg were cut, and special guards were placed along the railroad line. He transferred at Philadelphia, and finally reached the national capital without harm.

PIVOT IN THE UNION CAUSE

When the Civil War came, "Pennsylvania was the pivot on which the Union cause turned," according to historian Dr. S.K. Stevens.

It has been estimated that 80 percent of the war equipment used by Union forces came from Pennsylvania. Camp Curtin at Harrisburg was one of the great troop concentration centers of the Civil War. When President Lincoln first called for volunteers, enough men responded to make up twenty-five regiments instead of the fourteen requested. At a critical point in the war, Governor Curtin strengthened Lincoln's hand by calling a meeting of northern governors at Altoona and persuading them to go along with Lincoln's policies.

Altogether, more than 360,000 troops from Pennsylvania saw service in the Civil War. Of these, more than 33,000 died.

Pennsylvania was the only northern state in which a critical battle of the war was fought.

The first Confederate invasion of Pennsylvania was a brilliant cavalry maneuver by dashing General J.E.B. (Jeb) Stuart. On October 9, 1862, Stuart cut up through and past Chambersburg to destroy a railroad bridge, but he did not have time to destroy the structure. Making a big circle, he swung around a Union army and entered Maryland by the Emmitsburg Road. He took very little in civilian goods, but did seize as many as fifteen hundred horses.

Confederate General Robert E. Lee was aware of what might be gained by a full-scale invasion of Pennsylvania. Harrisburg was the chief center of the North's communications with the Southern front and for transport to the Army of the Potomac protecting Washington. If Pittsburgh or Philadelphia could be captured, the Union might even be forced out of the war.

General Lee decided to gamble, and began his invasion on June 15, 1863, through Waynesboro and Greencastle, swinging north and east to reach as far as Mechanicsburg and Wrightsville. Marching to oppose the invasion, the first large body of Union troops reached Gettysburg on July 1, and was attacked that day. As both sides brought up more and more reinforcements, this became one of the decisive battles of all time—the Battle of Gettysburg.

The battle is said to have been really three different battles in the "conflicts of three distinct days, each of which takes rank with the first battles of the world." On the third day the Union cannons stopped firing. General Lee thought the Union's ammunition was used up, and ordered General George E. Pickett to attack the Union forces. The Union cannons ended their silence, and a terrible artillery barrage struck Pickett's men. Only a few were able to penetrate the Union lines, and they were thrown back with terrible losses.

"The Union soldier fought at Gettysburg as he never had before. Often outnumbered at a given moment they fought with a tenacity and skill which amazed the Confederates." General Hancock, wounded commander of the corps attacked by Pickett, sent a message to General George G. Meade: "Troops under my command have repulsed the enemy's assault and we have gained a great victory. The enemy is now flying in all directions in my front."

On the fourth day it rained. "The rain, like sorrow, became torrential. It drowned the wounded and washed open the shallow graves of the dead." Although Lee expected a counterattack, it did not

The Battle of Gettysburg, Pennsylvania, July 3, 1863, *by Currier and Ives.*

come, and he was able to withdraw the remainder of his forces to the south. General Lee had lost his gamble.

"Two armies of brothers left twenty-five square miles around Gettysburg filled with dead and maimed. In three days 160,000 men fought in this battle. Fifty thousand were killed or wounded."

A third of the Union troops who fought at Gettysburg were from Pennsylvania, as was the Union commander, General Meade.

In analyzing the Civil War, many historians have declared that the three-day Battle of Gettysburg was the "turning point in the struggle to save the Union."

Under the leadership of David Wills a move was made by the state to purchase the land of the Gettysburg battlefield for a National

44

Cemetery. When the cemetery was to be dedicated, Wills at the last minute invited President Lincoln to "set apart these grounds to their sacred use by a few appropriate remarks."

Those "remarks" have become one of the best-known utterances of mankind—Lincoln's famed Gettysburg Address.

The last action of the Civil War in Pennsylvania occurred on July 30, 1864, when Confederate General Jubal Early raided Chambersburg and burned the city when the citizens refused to pay $100,000 ransom to save their community.

Late in the war a strange episode took place near Bloomsburg. Word came that draft deserters had fortified a spot on Fishing Creek Valley. A thousand Union soldiers were sent. One of them wrote, "Well do we remember the heroic charge . . . on the supposed battlements after a fortnight's preparation . . . and quite vivid is the picture . . . of the disgusted countenances as they reached the summit . . . and found not a man. . . . In a word . . . such a thing as a confederacy to resist the Federal Government never existed in Columbia County."

LAST OF A CENTURY

In the reconstruction period which followed the Civil War, a congressman from Pennsylvania was one of the leading figures. This was Thaddeus Stevens, a congressman who had a tremendous amount of power and influence in the country.

The people of Pennsylvania, bitter because of the sufferings of the war, approved some harsh measures after the war. This feeling did not last long in Pennsylvania, however, and the commonwealth soon returned to its traditional moderation.

In 1873 a new constitution was adopted by Pennsylvania. Three years later Philadelphia celebrated the hundredth anniversary of the Declaration of Independence with the great Centennial Exposition. This was the first large world's fair ever held in the United States. Thirty-eight foreign nations and thirty-nine states and territories had exhibits. There were 180 buildings on the grounds at Fairmount

Park. Many wonders of a new age were shown, including the telephone. Alexander Graham Bell exhibited his incredible new device at the fair, and everyone was astounded.

The American Federation of Labor was organized at Pittsburgh in 1881. In 1883 Sunbury became the first city in the world to be lighted by a three-wire central station incandescent electric system, built by Thomas Edison.

Heavy rains in May, 1889, broke the South Fork Dam above Johnstown. A wall of water 75 feet (22.86 meters) high and a half-mile (.8 kilometer) wide swept down on the unsuspecting city. In one of the great disasters of American history 2,200 lives were lost.

MODERN PENNSYLVANIA

The census of 1900 showed Pennsylvania with a population of 6,302,115. For the first time, more Pennsylvania people lived in cities than in the country.

In 1918 the 28th Division of the United States Army, which had been the 28th Pennsylvania National Guard Division, found itself in the path of the German's last big offensive of World War I, and stood its ground in the second battle of the Marne. The division fought with distinction for the rest of the war. More than 660,000 Pennsylvanians served in the war. Almost 3,000 manufacturing firms in the commonwealth provided necessary supplies through war contracts. The shipyards of Philadelphia and Chester were particularly important. The American Friends Service Committee, a Quaker organization, engaged in relief activities all around the world.

Once again, in 1926, Pennsylvania remembered the anniversary of American Independence, this time with a Sesqui-Centennial (150th anniversary) Exposition, also in Philadelphia as the first had been.

Ten years later, in 1936, Pennsylvania suffered the worst state-wide floods in its history. In that same year the national Democratic convention was held in Philadelphia, and Franklin Delano Roosevelt was nominated there and later elected president for the second time.

An eighth of the total population of Pennsylvania served in the armed forces during World War II—1,200,000 men and women in all. Only New York provided more. In this war 130 generals and admirals came from Pennsylvania, and there were forty army and navy installations in the commonwealth. In total production of wartime materiel Pennsylvania ranked sixth among the states. By war's end there were 33,000 Pennsylvanians dead. Thirty-five Pennsylvanians received the Congressional Medal of Honor for outstanding valor during the war.

In 1950, during the Korean conflict, and in the 1960s, during the Vietnam War, Pennsylvania people were again in military service.

In 1965, the new museum and archives building at Harrisburg was dedicated to William Penn.

In 1971, Pennsylvania adopted a state income tax.

Hurricane Agnes in 1972 caused the worst storm and flood damage in the state's history. Hurricane Eloise in 1975 caused great damage as well.

Also in that year the commonwealth dropped from third to fourth in national population rank and was expected to drop to sixth by 1980.

The outbreak of a strange disease at the American Legion convention in Philadelphia in 1976 attracted world attention, and has so far not been completely explained.

The year 1977 brought another Johnstown flood. Nearly a hundred lives were lost and there was widespread property damage.

Pennsylvania today has one of the most cosmopolitan populations of all the states, with Irish, German, Scandinavian, eastern European, southern European, and many other ethnic groups. New black citizens are coming to Pennsylvania in increasing numbers. Yet it may be said that "Pennsylvania is still a state peopled largely by the original settlers' stock."

One of the most unusual distinctions of any state belongs to modern-day Pennsylvania: It has a larger number of cities and towns than any other state, by a considerable margin. These communities have preserved, possibly to a greater extent than anywhere else, the historic past beside the structures of a dynamic present.

Above: The Ruffed Grouse is the state bird of Pennsylvania.
Below: The beautiful Mountain Laurel is Pennsylvania's state flower.

Natural Treasures

A PRIMEVAL WONDERLAND

The earliest settlers found Pennsylvania a primeval wonderland, mostly covered with dense forests of locust, black walnut, hickory, maple, beech, birch, cherry, and conifers. Black bear, deer, wild turkey, and other game were common.

Happily today, in spite of three hundred years of clearing and lumbering, 65 percent of Pennsylvania is still covered with forest, in some areas with virgin timber. It is amazing but true that there is more game in Pennsylvania today than in the time of William Penn. This happy situation has come about largely through conservation efforts. Pennsylvania's Gifford Pinchot was one of the world's leading conservation figures, helping to lead the battle to save the American wilderness. One of the first conservationists was Penn himself, who suggested that one out of every five acres should be left in trees.

Pennsylvania has more state forests than all the other northeastern states combined. In addition to the state forests, there is the Allegheny National Forest. The Pennsylvania state tree is the hemlock, a majestic and valuable tree.

Whitetail deer, the state animal; squirrel; other smaller animals; and even rarer creatures such as the wildcat and the lobo wolf may still be found. Hunters ride to the hounds in such places as Chester County. Almost 7,000,000 acres (2,832,802 hectares) of the state are open to hunting in season.

Ruffed grouse, the state bird; majestic wild turkey; quail; pheasant; woodcock; and other game birds, song birds, and migrating flocks such as the great white swans—all are well known in the commonwealth. As many as ten thousand of the huge swans have been counted on Lake Pymatuning. Bird lovers bought Hawk Mountain to preserve the graceful birds from hunters. Something about the wind currents of the mountain has made it a favorite spot for swooping and diving hawks.

Perch, catfish, sunfish, pike, shad running up the Delaware to spawn, and four kinds of trout all help to make up the fish popula-

Mallard duck and carp at the Lake Pymatuning spillway.

tion of Pennsylvania. A favorite sight for visitors is the mass of carp which crowd around the Lake Pymatuning spillway to have bread tossed their way. They huddle so close in the water that ducks have been known to walk across their backs to grab for the bread. Fishing in such rivers as the Susquehanna and the many fine trout streams delights thousands of anglers.

In spring the beautiful state flower, mountain laurel, blankets the hillsides in some areas. Columbine, arbutus, gentian, hepatica, orchis, whorled pogonia, passion flower, and rare lady slippers grow in the woodlands. One of the country's rarest plants is the box huckleberry. Some authorities feel these may be as much as ten thousand years old; the age is determined by the length of the root, which sometimes grows to incredible length.

MINERAL WEALTH WITHOUT MEASURE

The extent of commercially valuable mineral deposits is so large that Pennsylvania is one of the leading states in minerals. The bituminous coal beds of western Pennsylvania are almost continuous, some of them as thick as 3,500 feet (1,066.8 meters). Most of the nation's anthracite coal is found in Pennsylvania. Building stone, iron ore, oil, and gas all add to the mineral wealth. Gibbsville conglomerate, a rare stone formation found only in Pennsylvania, delights the geologist. The Morgantown and Cornwall ore banks are the most important sources of magnetite ore in the country. Three of the hills of the region are almost 50 percent metal.

People Use Their Treasures

MAKERS OF MANY THINGS

Although less glamorous than the gold of California or Alaska, the minerals of Pennsylvania have proved far more valuable over the years.

The world's leading industry had its beginning in Pennsylvania. The Seneca Indians skimmed an oil from the surface of the water and used it as medicine. Samuel M. Kier became the world's first commercial oil man by bottling and selling such oil for medicine. When a group of New England businessmen decided that oil might be used for illumination, they asked Edwin L. Drake to drill or dig a well to produce oil. This had never been done before, although some oil had been found in wells drilled for salt brine. Using crude tools, he sank a hole and lined it with cast-iron pipe. On August 27, 1859, at 69 feet (21.03 meters), oil was found.

This was the world's first oil well and the beginning of the industry that powers most of the engines of the world, lubricates most of the wheels and gears, and heats many of the houses and factories.

Drake's Well, near Titusville (below), was the world's first oil well.

Many small Pennsylvania communities became boom towns almost overnight. Pithole, one of the most famous, lasted only one year. For years Pennsylvania was the center of the world oil industry. The Oil City exchange controlled the price of oil for a long period. Oil business cleared through Oil City totaled a billion and a half dollars in the one year of 1885. At one time Pennsylvania oil men bragged that they would drink every drop of oil ever found west of the Mississippi River. That time is long past, and Pennsylvania no longer ranks among the top ten oil states, though oil and gas production remain important in Pennsylvania today.

The iron ore of Pennsylvania forms the most extensive banks in this country east of Lake Superior. The Cornwall Iron Mine began operations in 1732. From the richest anthracite coal mines in the world comes the bulk of the country's hard coal. Total production of anthracite and bituminous coal gives Pennsylvania fourth rank in coal among the states. Pennsylvania's cement industry at one time produced over half of the United States total. It still produces a large amount. The slate quarries at Bangor have produced as much as two-thirds of the country's roof slate in a given year. Other stone, natural gas, fire clay, and lime are additional important Pennsylvania minerals. For many years, Pennsylvania has ranked fifth or sixth among the states in mineral production.

Pennsylvania production of steel—the world's basic material—leads by far all other states, and this in one of the two greatest steel-producing countries of the world. This tremendous industry has grown from the first iron forge established by Thomas Potts and Thomas Rutter in 1716 on Manatawny Creek.

Pittsburgh pioneered in another basic industry—aluminum—and Pennsylvania remains one of the leading aluminum-producing states.

Manufacturing pioneers have been plentiful in Pennsylvania. The famed Conestoga wagon, which played a leading part in winning the West, was first manufactured on the banks of Conestoga Creek. Its boatlike construction was designed to prevent shifting of the loads, which might weigh eight tons (7.25 metric tons), and to aid in crossing streams. The wheels were wide to permit travel on soggy ground.

Conestoga Wagon on a Pennsylvania Pike in 1814, *by Thomas Birch. These wagons were invented by the Pennsylvania Dutch.*

The "Kentucky" rifle originated in Pennsylvania. Martin Meylin and the Pennsylvania gunsmiths were 125 years ahead of their time in inventing and producing this brilliantly successful weapon. The details of its construction in the shops around Lancaster are fascinating. Barrels were forged from iron bars in charcoal fires and rifled on primitive wooden machines. They were welded from the center to both ends in order to "run out the devil." The reputation of many a soldier and frontiersman—including Daniel Boone—often was made with the use of the Pennsylvania rifle.

Pennsylvania also pioneered in piano manufacture. The first American pianoforte was built at Philadelphia in 1775.

The nation's first nuclear power plant was opened at Shippingport.

Captain John B. Ford is called "the father of the plate glass industry in America." Pittsburgh Plate Glass Company at Ford City has the largest plant of its kind in the world. Matthias Baldwin, jeweler turned locomotive maker, created one of the world's leading locomotive works in Pennsylvania. Textiles, clothing, food products, leather goods, and electrical machinery are all important in Pennsylvania industry. Pennsylvania ranks sixth among the states in manufacturing.

53

Paced by the careful farming methods of Pennsylvania Germans, Pennsylvania has long been a leading agricultural state. Eighty-eight thousand farms today produce crops annually worth over a billion dollars. By order of value, principal crops are hay, corn, wheat, oats, potatoes, apples, tobacco, and vegetables.

Near the town of Northeast is the longest continuous planting of grapes in the world—10,000 acres (4,046.86 hectares). Pennsylvania leads all states in mushroom production, with about 70 percent of the nation's supply coming from the Longwood area. More importantly, Pennsylvania is first in the production of frozen dairy products. It has the largest manufacturing plants in the world for processing package ice cream, apple juice, and grape juice.

In 1860 Pennsylvania became the country's largest producer of timber. While timber leadership has moved to western states, Pennsylvania still manufactures wood products valued at several hundred million dollars each year.

TRANSPORTATION AND COMMUNICATION

Pennsylvania has been a pioneer in transportation and communication from very early times. In 1790, years before Robert Fulton's success, inventor John Fitch was operating a steamboat on a regular run between Philadelphia and Burlington, New Jersey.

The first crushed stone road in the United States, the country's first turnpike—Philadelphia to Lancaster—opened in 1794. The Pennsylvania Turnpike, first opened in 1940, became America's original superhighway.

The first steam locomotive on rails in America operated out of Honesdale on an experimental basis in 1829. By 1834 Pennsylvania had 300 miles (482.8 kilometers) of railroad, a fourth of the total mileage in the whole country at that time.

Pennsylvania's amazing canal system was begun in 1797 with the Conewago Canal. A combination of canals and rails to reach over the mountains from Philadelphia to Pittsburgh was begun in 1826. An ingenious "portage railroad" carried canal boats over the Allegheny

The Allegheny Mountain Tunnel (left) is one of Pennsylvania's many tunnels that simplify travel through the mountains.
Below: Portage Railroad, by George Storm. This railroad was once used to carry canal boats over the Alleghenies from Philadelphia to Pittsburgh.

Mountains between the canal terminals at Hollidaysburg and Johnstown.

Today tremendous "three way" traffic flows down the Ohio, over the Great Lakes, and up the Delaware. The port of Philadelphia and the other Delaware ports handle the second greatest volume of shipping of any single port area in the United States.

The first complete Bible printed in America came from the press of Christopher Sauer at Germantown. The famous trial of printer Peter Zenger at Philadelphia in 1734 was especially important in maintaining a free press in America. The growth of publishing in Pennsylvania was amazing. Pennsylvania's first newspaper was begun in 1719 as the *American Weekly Mercury.* Philadelphia early became a center for the development of magazines, including the *Saturday Evening Post,* said to have been founded by Benjamin Franklin; *Graham's Magazine;* and *Godey's Lady's Book.* Philadelphia has also been a center of the music-publishing industry.

Some of the earliest feature movies were made at Betzwood, including the first "spectacle," the *Battle of Shiloh,* produced by Sigmund Lubin. On June 19, 1905, the world's first all-motion-picture nickelodeon opened in Pittsburgh.

The world's first commercial broadcasting station, KDKA, began transmission at Pittsburgh on November 2, 1920.

A section of the Pennsylvania Turnpike, America's original superhighway.

Human Treasures

FRANKLIN: A HARMONIOUS MULTITUDE

On his death at the age of eighty-four, the world mourned one of its most notable citizens. Twenty thousand people—the largest crowd in the history of Philadelphia to that time—turned out for his funeral. This was Benjamin Franklin, first citizen of Philadelphia and one of the most extraordinary men America has ever produced.

He found America a struggling group of wilderness communities; he left it well on its way to being a strongly united world power. He found it a backward, poor, and narrow place; he left it stirred with a knowledge and feeling for every branch of learning and culture and with the roots of most of its future progress in the science and humanities. An amazing amount of this vast progress during the "Age of Franklin" must be credited to the tireless efforts and phenomenal brilliance of Dr. Benjamin Franklin.

To list his accomplishments would take more space than is available here. He achieved outstanding success in a dozen fields—any one of which might have occupied other men for a lifetime. After a successful career in business, he turned to the many subjects that interested him more: scientific discovery, government, and diplomacy; in each of these he became the very symbol of a new age of enlightenment.

As a printer and publisher of books, newspapers, and magazines, he first gained fame for his *Poor Richard's Almanack,* published annually for twenty-five years. From that point on, his vast outpouring as an author of scientific studies, letters, and books would alone have given him a lasting reputation.

As a scientist and inventor his work made him internationally famous. He helped to establish the nature of lightning and electricity with his famous kite experiment and many others. His scientific genius soon won him worldwide fame and the respect of scholars everywhere. He invented the Franklin stove, bifocal eyeglasses, the lightning rod, and many other devices. He suggested the possibility of vaccination for smallpox and diagnosed the causes of lead poison-

Painting of Benjamin Franklin by Constantino Brumidi.

ing. He even wrote a best-selling book, *Every Man His Own Doctor.*

Another complete career was devoted to public and community service. He was official printer to the colony of Pennsylvania. He was mainly responsible for the paving of Philadelphia's streets, better street lighting, the organization of fire companies, the first circulating library in the country, Philadelphia's first hospital, and scientific institutions. He helped to establish the forerunners of the University of Pennsylvania, and was the deputy postmaster general of the colonies for twenty-one years. America's first expedition to the Arctic in 1753 to explore for a Northwest Passage came largely through his influence.

His greatest fame came as an international statesman and molder of governments. He proposed the Albany plan to unite the colonies. Although this was not accepted, it was the beginning of the idea of union. Franklin represented several of the colonies in England. When war came he was a member of the Continental Congress, became first postmaster general, tried to persuade the Canadians to join the colonies to the south, and was one of the five who wrote the Declaration of Independence. Possibly his greatest contribution to the Revolutionary War was to win France as an American ally.

Norman Wilkinson says, "Franklin, the universal man, simple in dress, modest in manner, benign, witty and charming in conversation, captured the affection of the French from the sophisticates of the salon to the peasant." At the end of the war he was a commissioner in writing the peace treaty. Wilkinson continues, "It is to the shrewd 'Poor Richard' that America is indebted for the very favorable terms of the peace treaty . . . September, 1783."

His last great service to country and world, when he was ill and growing old, was to give the benefit of his advice and counsel in the creation of the government of the United States—the Constitution.

The last few years of his life passed pleasantly for him though he was in very poor health. His mind remained as alert as ever until the end came on April 17, 1790.

"No other town burying its great men ever buried more of itself than Philadelphia with Franklin," says Carl Van Doren. "Yet," adds Wilkinson, "after a century and a half he remains Philadelphia's first citizen."

MIGHTIER THAN THE SWORD

William Penn has been called "America's greatest colonizer," "noblest figure among the colonial governors and proprietors." Thomas Jefferson went much further in his praise, to call Penn the "greatest lawgiver the world has produced."

He was a man of religious sincerity and yet a man of the world, a polished courtier, and protégé of the Duke of York, who later became King James II. Although thrown in prison six times because of his Quaker religious beliefs, whipped and disowned by his father, and expelled from Oxford, William Penn never hesitated to put his beliefs into action.

Given land in America, Penn started his noble experiment to furnish asylum for the persecuted in the old countries, and to provide an opportunity for putting his advanced theories of government into practice. These ideas are best explained in the preface to his *First Frame of Government.*

Penn was the first to propose that the American colonies should unite, and he also drew up plans for an international organization with ideals and structure similar to the United Nations, which came into being more than 250 years later.

He was a warm and friendly man. At his beloved home, Pennsbury, near Philadelphia, "The great hall in front, large enough to accommodate whole delegations of callers, and the dining room, whose long board creaked under a plenitude of beef, mutton, pork, smoked shad, imported claret and madeira, Indian corn and English peas, tell us that here was the open-hearted hospitable Penn." The Indians could pay no higher compliment than to say a man was like William Penn. When he returned to England in 1701, the Indians had James Logan write a letter to the king: "We the Kings and Sachems of the Ancient Nations of the Suswuehannah and Shavanah Indians . . . can do no less than acknowledge that he has

Pennsbury Manor, William Penn's home in Bucks County, Pennsylvania.

been not only always just but very kind to us as well as our ancient Kings and Sachems deceased . . . not suffering us to receive any wrong . . . giving us his house for our home . . . and freely entertaining us at his own cost and often filling us with many presents of necessary goods. . . . We could say much more of his good council and instructions. . . . But let this suffice to the great King, in love to our good friend and brother, William Penn.''

Death came to Proprietor William Penn in England, far from his beloved Philadelphia, on July 30, 1718. "His greatest achievement was the message that . . . men are bound together by more than selfish interests, that the mutual tolerance of men of good conscience is the basis of all human dealing. This message will have meaning as long as life endures."

MEN OF IRON

Many later day "proprietors" of Pennsylvania have made their mark in business and industry. Andrew Carnegie began work at the age of thirteen for $1.20 a week. He created the Carnegie Steel Company, which became the first billion dollar industry—United States Steel. Carnegie gave more than $350,000,000 to charity and made his name a household word for "giving."

Charles M. Schwab was called the world's greatest salesman. He was another of the "iron men." He had the idea for consolidating a great empire and calling it United States Steel. He later built the Bethlehem Steel Company.

Henry Clay Frick became the largest producer of coal and coke in the world and also gave the world the huge Frick art collection.

Andrew Mellon helped organize and finance some of the modern industrial giants, including Gulf Oil, the Aluminum Company of America, and the Carborundum Company. His mammoth art collection and his contributions formed the basis for the National Gallery of Art at Washington, D. C.

Inventor and industrialist George Westinghouse built a great electrical empire in Pennsylvania.

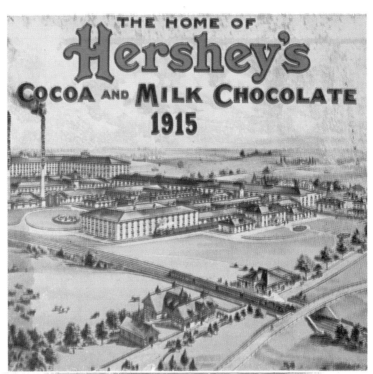

One of the world's most interesting business activities was created by Milton S. Hershey, who built the town of Hershey on the success of his Hershey bars. He established the city of Hershey as a model community with every comfort and cultural advantage for his workers and made Pennsylvania the world leader in the chocolate business.

F. W. Woolworth began his chain of novelty stores at Lancaster. John Wanamaker was another Pennsylvania merchant whose name is known around the world. Stores have long sold the products of another Pennsylvanian, Henry J. Heinz, whose "fifty-seven varieties" of pickles, beans, and other canned foodstuff are known everywhere.

Pennsylvania inventors and scientists include Daniel Drawbaugh, who, some claim, invented a workable telephone ten years before Alexander Graham Bell; Joseph Saxton, of Huntingdon, "father of photography in America"; Philip Syng Physick, called "father of American surgery"; Isaac Hays, who pioneered in the study of astigmatism and color blindness; and Dr. Joseph Priestley, discoverer of oxygen and carbon dioxide. The latter led, among other things, to soda pop. Lewis David van Schweinitz and John Bartram, renowned botanists, and Edward D. Cope, known for his work in paleontology, are other prominent scientists.

IN PUBLIC SERVICE

America's only bachelor president, James Buchanan, born near Mercersburg, was the only president to date to come from Pennsylvania. He served as a United States congressman and senator, minister to Russia, secretary of state under Polk, and minister to England before he became the fifteenth president in 1857.

Another American president was an adopted Pennsylvanian— Dwight D. Eisenhower, whose name means "the one who strikes with iron." His affection for the community of Gettysburg and his home there are well known.

Albert Gallatin, of New Geneva, served as secretary of the treasury under Jefferson and Madison. In later life he studied and wrote; he considered his Indian studies his most valuable work. Simon Cameron and Edwin M. Stanton, both of Pennsylvania, were the first and second secretaries of war under Lincoln.

Governor Andrew G. Curtin, "the soldiers' friend," with Governor Oliver P. Morton of Indiana, was one of the two most influential of all state governors during the Civil War. Another prominent governor was Gifford Pinchot.

BEAUTIFUL DREAMER

Only three musicians are in the Hall of Fame for Great Americans at New York University. One is Stephen Collins Foster, born on the Fourth of July, 1826, at Lawrenceville, now part of Pittsburgh. His genius captured in melody and words an important period of American history.

His first published work, "Open Thy Lattice, Love," was written when he was seventeen. In his brief life he wrote more than two hundred songs and compositions. Not very successful financially, his life ended at the age of only thirty-seven, and he had only thirty-eight cents in a small purse. With the coins was a note bearing the scrawled words "Dear friends and gentle hearts." This may have been the beginning of a new song, which again showed the human feeling of this remarkable artist. He was buried in Allegheny Cemetery at Pittsburgh.

Stephen Foster's work, however, lives on. Who can forget such songs as "Old Folks at Home," "My Old Kentucky Home," "Old Black Joe," "Massa's in de Cold, Cold Ground," "Come Where My Love Lies Dreaming," "Oh! Susanna," "Camptown Races," "Nelly Was a Lady," and "Old Dog Tray"? His last song, "Beautiful Dreamer," was his masterpiece, and was not published until two months after his death.

Other composers from Pennsylvania include Samuel Barber, Peter Mennin, Ethelbert Nevin, and Charles Wakefield Cadman. Henry T. Burleigh is one of the most important black composers of recent years. Conrad Beissel composed 491 hymns. Composer Victor Herbert also conducted the Pittsburgh Symphony. Singers Marian Anderson, John Charles Thomas, and Nelson Eddy all have Pennsylvania roots. Leopold Stokowski, Eugene Ormandy, William Steinberg, and Fred Waring gained fame as conductors of widely differing groups of "Pennsylvanians."

Andrew Wyeth is Pennsylvania's most famous contemporary artist.

Other well-known Pennsylvania artists are Maxfield Parrish and Benjamin West. West, born in Swarthmore, went to England and became a friend of King George III. West openly defended the American colonies before the monarch. Jacob Eichholtz was a copper worker who became a fine artist, known especially for his portraits of Thaddeus Stevens and President Buchanan.

Because of his reputation for dramatic paintings of historical subjects, Peter Frederick Rothermel was chosen to do the great paintings of the Battle of Gettysburg now hanging in the State Museum. Violet Oakley has been called Pennsylvania's greatest woman artist. William Rush is known as the first American sculptor. Another noted sculptor was George Gray Barnard, born in Bellefonte.

These United States postage stamps honor three famous Pennsylvanians: Artists Mary Cassatt *(above)* and Thomas Eakins *(left)* and financier Haym Salomon *(below).*

Among notable modern sculptors are the three Calder brothers, all with first names of Alexander.

"First American novelist of distinction" is a common description of Charles Brockden Brown, 1771-1810. Stephen Vincent Benet, Christopher Morley, Ida M. Tarbell, Kate Douglas Wiggin, who wrote *Rebecca of Sunnybrook Farm,* and Mary Roberts Rinehart all are writers claimed by Pennsylvania.

WARTIME LEADERS

General "Mad" Anthony Wayne, born in Chester County, was the "troubleshooter of the Revolution." Sixteen United States counties have been named in Wayne's honor, as well as numerous towns and a university.

Arthur St. Clair of Greensburg was a successful Revolutionary War general. As president of the Continental Congress, St. Clair was, in effect, actually a "president" of the country, although not officially a president of the United States.

Pennsylvania's Civil War leaders included Admiral David D. Porter and Generals George B. McClellan, George G. Meade, Winfield S. Hancock, John F. Reynolds, John W. Geary, and John F. Hartranft.

As chief of staff of the United States, General George Catlett Marshall, a native of Uniontown, gained fame as one of the leading military figures of World War II. Marshall later became secretary of state under President Truman. General H.H. "Hap" Arnold was born in Gladwyne, and James "Slim Jim" Gavin of Mount Carmel was the youngest major general of the World War II army. Generals Alexander M. Patch and Lyman L. Lemnitzer and Admirals Harold R. Stark and Thomas C. Kinkaid were other prominent wartime figures.

Indian leaders include Chief Cornplanter, who worked out peace treaties after the Revolution. Today only a small Indian settlement remains on Pennsylvania grounds granted to Cornplanter. Another notable chief was Half King Tanacharison, the dynamic Seneca leader. Famed Mingo Chief James Logan of Rochester was known because of the massacre of his family by white settlers. He was a son of Chief Shikellamy.

SUCH INTERESTING PEOPLE

In 1728 Mordecai Lincoln, great-great-grandfather of Abraham Lincoln, was Pennsylvania's commissioner for defense against the Indians. Conrad Weiser was known as a "master of Indian diplomacy." Prince Demetrius Augustine Gallitzin became a missionary on the Pennsylvania frontier in 1795. Swedish Reverend John Campanius, first missionary to the Delaware Indians in Pennsylvania, was known for his translations of the catechism and parts of the Bible into Indian languages.

Misfortune in old age came to a number of noted Pennsylvanians. Robert Morris, financier of the Revolution, served time in a debtors' prison. Wealthy Baron Steigel died penniless. Toward the end he worked as a janitor in the church built by funds he had donated at the height of his prosperity. The annual payment of one rose, which he requested from the church, is still being made. Henry Eckford and Noah Brown, builders of the Erie fleet, both became impoverished. At the age of seventy, Brown was found working as a journeyman in a shipyard. John Sutter, on whose land gold was found, and who once owned much of California, was ruined when his properties were overrun by gold seekers. He moved to Lititz in 1870 and was buried there in 1880.

Robert E. Peary, first man at the North Pole, was born near Ebensburg. John Green, buried at Bristol, was captain of the first American ship to sail around the world, in 1787-1790.

Richard Allen was the founder of the African Methodist Church at Philadelphia. The strange career of United States Marine Faustin Wirkus included a period as "king" of the island of La Gonave, near Haiti. An earlier ruler named Faustin had prophesied that another Faustin would come to rule over the inhabitants, so they accepted Wirkus at once.

An oil-tinted Matthew Brady photograph of Thaddeus Stevens, a congressman who was a leader in the Congressional reconstruction plan during the period following the Civil War.

Charlotte Este overheard her father and British officers plotting to capture General George Washington. She worked her way through British lines and may have saved Washington's life. Another Revolutionary War figure was Christopher Ludwig, baker-general of the Revolution, who persuaded a large number of Hessian troops to desert. Betsy Ross, who gained fame as the maker of our first flag, was a real person, though the flag story is now generally regarded as a legend.

George Rapp was the religious leader who founded both Harmony and Economy. Solomon Spaulding wrote *Manuscript Found,* considered by some to be the basis of the *Book of Mormon.* Dr. Caspar Wistar gave his name to the Wisteria vine.

Entertainers and theatrical people of Pennsylvania have included the Drew and Barrymore families; Princess Grace of Monaco, formerly Grace Kelly; the Warner Brothers; Edwin Forrest; Perry Como; W.C. Fields; and Vaughn Monroe. Baseball player Christy Mathewson was a native of Factoryville.

Teaching and Learning

The institution now called the University of Pennsylvania was the only nondenominational college of the colonies. It was begun as an academy and became the College of Philadelphia; given status as the university of the commonwealth in 1789, it took its present name in 1791. During the Revolution, the confiscation of sixty Tory estates formed the basis for the university's endowment fund.

Pennsylvania State University is another leading commonwealth institution. The commonwealth's land-grant college at State College must be considered one of the finest of its kind. Its College of Mineral Industries is well known.

The University of Pittsburgh's skyscraper headquarters is known as the "forty-two-story little red schoolhouse." An unusual feature of that university is its "nationality" classrooms, designed to represent different countries, and furnished by various nationality groups.

The "forty-two-story little red schoolhouse," headquarters of the University of Pittsburgh.

Among the approximately 130 universities and colleges of Pennsylvania are such other well-known names as Bryn Mawr and Villanova at Bryn Mawr; Bucknell University, Lewisburg; Wilson College, Chambersburg; Lincoln University, Avondale; the Quaker College of Haverford; Duquesne University, Pittsburgh; Swarthmore at Swarthmore. Washington and Jefferson College at Washington, founded in 1780, is the oldest institution of higher education west of the Alleghenies.

Franklin and Marshall College, Lancaster, was named for Benjamin Franklin and Chief Justice John Marshall.

Pennsylvania has fine scientific institutions. Franklin Institute, endowed by Franklin and founded in 1824, is a fine scientific and technical institution. The Mellon Institute and the Carnegie Institute of Technology are other fine schools bearing the names of their donors. Dr. John Morgan founded America's first school of medicine at Philadelphia in 1765. The Council of Science and Technology helps industry to find and obtain scientific services, materials, and personnel.

The Philadelphia Academy of Fine Arts is America's oldest art museum and school. The International Correspondence School in Scranton is known as the "world's schoolhouse." The Training School of the Pennsylvania Game Commission, near Brockway, was the first of its kind in the country.

Pennsylvania's first school was founded early in the 1640s in the Swedish settlement of Tinicum. The first public school system was organized at Philadelphia in 1689. The Quaker concern with education was that "Their youth shall come in contact with teachers who have character as well as knowledge to share with their pupils." Education took a great stride forward in 1834 with the act for free public schools, advocated by Governor George Wolf, Timothy Pickering, Samuel Breck, and Thaddeus Stevens, whose eloquence saved it from repeal.

Today the public, private, parochial and independent, elementary, and secondary schools, along with the institutions of higher education and graduate studies, provide a splendid system of education for the commonwealth.

Enchantment of Pennsylvania

WHERE LIBERTY PEALED

Metropolitan Philadelphia blends some of the magnificent portions of our heritage with some of the most dynamic aspects of modern American culture. Visitors to Valley Forge today may feel that they are stepping into history.

And yet, not far from where a ragged American army drilled barefoot in the snow two hundred years ago, the Valley Forge Space Technology Center undertook development of a military spaceship, the Manned Orbital Laboratory.

Perhaps the best way to become acquainted with Philadelphia, once the second-largest city of the English speaking world, is from a high spot such as the Penn Mutual's rooftop observatory. From this spot there is a spectacular bird's-eye view of the vast city.

Off to the south and west are the huge Philadelphia naval base, International airport, and one of the large "sea theaters," the Aquarama, with its show of marine life. To the east, the oldest religious structure in Pennsylvania, Gloria Dei Church, pierces the blanket of trees. The blue ribbon of the historic Delaware River makes the border between Pennsylvania and New Jersey. Clustered closer below are some of the most hallowed buildings of American history. Many of them can be visited on a walking tour.

Philadelphia has provided the twenty-two-acre (nine-hectare) Independence National Historical Park as a setting for some of America's most historic buildings.

A tree-shaded walk leads through the park to the south side of the building many consider to be America's greatest shrine—the old Pennsylvania Statehouse, now called Independence Hall. Inside, old and young alike can pause to remember the patriots, who after struggling with their consciences in the spacious assembly hall, finally gathered to sign the Declaration of Independence, placing a few colonies on the way to becoming a great republic.

A graceful archway in Independence Hall once led to that now-silent "Voice of America," the Liberty Bell, which has now been moved to its own pavilion nearby. It was a sultry July day when its deep voice called the people of Philadelphia to hear the first public reading of that declaration. When the British took Philadelphia, the Liberty Bell was moved to Allentown for safety. Brought back to Philadelphia, it tolled on many occasions, until it cracked in 1835 while being rung during the funeral of Chief Justice John Marshall.

In the park at night glow fifty-six gas lamps—one for each signer of the Declaration of Independence. On summer nights the "Lumadrama," *The American Bell,* is presented. This is a spectacle of light and sound with words by Archibald MacLeish, narration by Fredric March, and music by members of the Philadelphia Symphony.

Close to Independence Hall is Christ Church, where Washington and many other leaders worshipped. This is one of America's most beautiful religious buildings. Not far away in Christ Church Burial Ground rests the great patriot-author-publisher-inventor-scientist-statesman Benjamin Franklin, beside his wife Deborah. On Arch Street is the home of Betsy Ross, where it was once thought the first American flag was made. Whether the tradition is true or not, the story has been responsible for preserving one of the best examples of a modest colonial home just as it once was.

In the neighborhood, also, is Carpenters' Hall, where patriots spoke and the First Continental Congress met. City Hall is a huge, impressive building. On its crest is the gigantic thirty-seven foot (eleven-meter) statue of William Penn, gazing fondly down on his city.

For contrast Philadelphia has created modern Center City, with its new skyscrapers gleaming in stainless steel and acres of glass, grouped with fine taste at Penn Center, hub of the city's business life. It begins at City Hall and stretches westward toward the Schuylkill River along the John F. Kennedy Boulevard.

The city-wide improvement program has cost Philadelphia billions of dollars, but it has rescued the city from aged eyesores and terrible traffic. A one-hundred-million-dollar food distribution center replaced the site of a city dump. Business life now flourishes, and historic shrines are once more placed in proper settings.

72

Among the many sights
of historic interest in
Philadelphia are the
Liberty Bell (left),
the Betsy Ross house
(bottom left), and Independence
Hall (bottom right).

The Franklin Institute is a science, educational, and research institution.

Philadelphia was once called the "Athens of America." In many ways it still deserves that title. Most notable in the field of culture is the Philadelphia Art Museum with its priceless collection. It crowns a wooded slope with a view of the Schuylkill River. The Philadelphia Symphony is one of the greatest of the world's great orchestras. American opera had its beginning in Philadelphia.

The heritage of independent research established by America's first great scientist, Benjamin Franklin, continues at the Franklin Institute. The great statue of Franklin is a notable feature of the Institute. Its museum interprets scientific facts in simple and dramatic form. Here, also, is the Fels Planetarium.

The Academy of Natural Sciences was the first natural history museum in the United States. Rodin Museum, University Museum, Philadelphia Art Alliance, Historical Society of Pennsylvania, American Swedish Historical Museum, Atwater Kent Museum of Philadelphia History, and the Philadelphia Academy of the Fine Arts are other fine institutions. The latter is the oldest art institution in the country. Almost every famous person in the history of music has appeared in the Academy of Music since it was built in 1857.

Everywhere are reminders that this is a city of United States "firsts": the first scientific society, the first circulating library, the first medical college, the first hospital, the first bank, the first daily newspaper, the first fire insurance company, the first chamber of commerce, among others.

America's first zoo was established in four thousand-acre (more than sixteen hundred-hectare) Fairmount Park. In the park is Robin Hood Dell where the Philadelphia Symphony plays its summer concerts under the stars, and the John B. Kelly Playhouse, with summer-long theater. In the park are preserved twenty-three historic houses, six of them open to the public, containing treasures of period furnishings.

Also in Philadelphia are a United States mint; St. George's Church, the oldest Methodist building in America; the John F. Kennedy Stadium, where the annual Army-Navy game is played; the Stephen Collins Foster Memorial; Congress Hall; Washington Square; the Friends Meeting house; the Edgar Allan Poe House; the Chapel of the Four Chaplains; the Trade and Convention Center; and the various colleges and universities of the area.

Old Saint Mary's Church, 1763, was the nation's first Roman Catholic Cathedral. Commodore John Barry, called "father of the United States Navy," is buried in its churchyard.

AROUND PHILADELPHIA

Within the circle of greater Philadelphia, also, is much of scenic and historic interest.

Almost on the eastern tip of Pennsylvania, William Penn's country home, Pennsbury Manor, has been restored as a fascinating reminder of the way of life of the period. In 1932 it was presented to the commonwealth by Warner County on the 250th anniversary of Penn's arrival in America. Its restoration was supervised by Dr. Donald A. Cadzow.

Levittown was one of the country's first planned and completely created suburban cities. Bryn Athyn Cathedral near Morrisville is the beautiful and impressive headquarters church for the Swedenborgian faith.

Washington Crossing State Park commemorates that historic crossing of the Delaware at the spot where it occurred. Dwight Eisenhower said, "I wish every schoolchild and every teacher could see the original of the famous Leutze painting of 'Washington Crossing the Delaware'—which is now housed in a fine new building . . . and hear the inspiring recorded narrative of that exploit."

A beautiful example of colonial architecture is Hope Lodge, restored and refurnished for all to see. The house is thought to have been built by Samuel Morris for his fiancee. However, he is said to have remarked "I have built the pen; now all I have to do is go to England, get the sow and start the litter." When this remark got back to his intended bride she changed her mind, and Morris died a bachelor at Hope Lodge.

Almost within Philadelphia city boundaries is Governor Printz Park, preserving the memories of Tinicum Island, the first permanent European settlement in Pennsylvania.

Brandywine battlefield is another Revolutionary War site of interest in Metropolitan Philadelphia.

Waynesborough, home of Anthony Wayne at Paoli, and St. David's Protestant Episcopal Church at Wayne are of interest. At St. David's, General Washington had the window sash weights removed and melted for bullets. Still preserved there is the ancient bass viol that accompanied the choir before the organ was installed.

One of the world's finest gardens is Longwood Gardens, west of Philadelphia. Its million and a half dollar conservatory ranks among the best. The water garden offers a spectacular five-acre (two-hectare) display of fountains. This is the former estate of chemical magnate Pierre S. du Pont.

OTHER EASTERN POINTS OF INTEREST

New Hope is known for its unusual colony of artists and writers. Spread over 4 acres (1.6 hectares) near Upper Black Eddy are the Ringing Rocks. When struck, they give out a bell-like tone, with the pitch depending on the size of the rock.

The foremost Moravian church in the United States is considered to be the Central Moravian Church at Bethlehem. It is famous for its trombone choir. The celebration of Christmas in Bethlehem is one of the best-known celebrations in the country. On South Mountain is a huge Star of Bethlehem, and the Christmas music is renowned. Bethlehem was one of the earliest American cultural centers; the finest music was often heard there before it came to other parts of the country.

One of the outstanding music events of the United States is the annual Bach Festival at Lehigh University in May.

Allentown was named "All-American City" in 1962. Its Art Museum has the Kress Memorial collection. During British occupation the Liberty Bell was hidden at Zion's Reformed Church, and a full-size replica is now on display in Liberty Bell Shrine there.

The Mercer Museum with its famous collection of tools of early trades was built by Dr. Henry C. Mercer without any plan, but just proceeded as he took the fancy. At the Audubon Wildlife Sanctuary in Montgomery County is the first American home of famed naturalist John James Audubon.

Pottsgrove, west of Pottstown, preserves the home of John Potts, pioneer Pennsylvania ironmaster. Hopewell Village is a restored eighteenth-century iron plantation, now a national historic site. Daniel Boone, famed frontiersman, was born southeast of Reading; his birthplace has been preserved as a Pennsylvania shrine.

Reading's fine Public Museum and Art Gallery is set in a twenty-five-acre (ten-hectare) aboretum. On Mount Penn, The Pagoda is a unique observation tower, once a hotel in Japanese style. It is anchored to the mountain with ten tons (nine metric tons) of bolts.

East of Lebanon is Conrad Weiser Memorial Park, named for the Pennsylvania ambassador to the Indians. West Grove observes its traditional gift of a rose each September to a descendant of William Penn, as a symbol of the rent to Penn. Ephrata Cloisters was the home of a religious group that sought to serve God in medieval fashion. The surviving buildings are open to the public.

One of the finest collections of rural Americana is found in the Pennsylvania Farm Museum north of Lancaster. Here 250,000 items show a history of farming in America. At the annual craft days here, all the old crafts flourish once again. Wheatland, home of President James Buchanan at Lancaster, has been completely restored.

York is sometimes called the "first capital of the United States," since the Articles of Confederation were adopted there by the Continental Congress. The historical society museum features a reproduction of a village square as in Revolutionary times.

Hershey was one of the world's first completely planned communities, based on the desire of M.S. Hershey to make his chocolate plant and community the best possible place to work and live. The cultural, sports, and recreational facilities he established are superb. Naturally, the two main streets are Cocoa and Chocolate Avenues. The Rose Garden has 42,000 plants, and the nearby Tulip Garden has 30,000 blooms in the spring. The extraordinary sports arena features professional hockey, basketball, ice skating, and shows.

Ephrata Cloisters, an eighteenth-century restored religious community.

At Carlisle is the grave of Revolutionary heroine Molly Pitcher.

Today, of course, the scene of the Battle of Gettysburg is a hallowed and protected national shrine. Here is the Eternal Light Peace Memorial, on Oak Ridge, dedicated by President Franklin D. Roosevelt to "Peace Eternal in a Nation United." The Pennsylvania State Monument at the battlefield contains the names of more than 34,500 Pennsylvania troops who took part in the battle. President Eisenhower's retirement farm adjoins the battlefield.

At Gettysburg, the National Museum is "the most visited battlefield museum in the world." Another museum is the Hall of Presidents with figures of all the presidents. The Lincoln Room Museum preserves the room in the Wills House where Lincoln worked on the Gettysburg Address.

Near Sunbury is Fort Augusta, one of the great stumbling blocks of French and Indian aggression. A large scale model is on display at the site of the fort, and there is a museum in the Hunter Mansion. Nearby, one of the Pennsylvania historic properties is the Dr. Joseph Priestley house. The American Chemical Society was organized there in 1876.

When anthracite coal mining began to fail at Scranton after World War II, the city completely reorganized and restored its economy. The Scranton plan has been used as a model by other communities since that time. In the city are the country's largest lace mills and the University of Scranton. The Everhart Museum of Natural History, Science and Art at Scranton has several outstanding collections.

WONDERFUL GOOD

The Pennsylvania Germans and their communities continue to be among the greatest attractions for visitors to Pennsylvania.

Their beliefs and philosophies cover a wide range. In some parts of Pennsylvania where there are many "Plain People" there may be more buggies than autos on the roads. Several Amish houses are open to visitors and give a good idea of their way of life. One of these is 6 miles (9.6 meters) east of Lancaster on Highway 30.

"An Amish Wedding,"
Kutztown Folk Festival.

This charming farm is operated complete with cows, pigs and horses, chickens, geese, and Guinea hens. Tobacco dries in the loft. The buggies are ready for use; the tools hang in the sheds. Inside, the house is just as an Amish home would be. Clothes hang from pegs in the wall; there are no closets. The beds have woven rope mattresses, with handsewn quilts.

According to Professor R.W. Gilbert, "The Pennsylvania Germans gave America an art which was colorful, decorative, simple, primitive but not necessarily crude, and which was dominated by geometrical balance and haunted by innumerable figures and motifs that have lost meaning through the years. . . It was a vital part of the greatest of all arts—the art of living. Even their tombstones show touches of artistry, perhaps symbolical of a life after death."

The interest of people in the culture of the Pennsylvania Germans continues to grow. The opportunities to observe this culture in its native setting rank high among the advantages of a trip to Pennsylvania. Originals and copies of their art and furniture are much in demand. Visitors are advised to "come hungry" to Pennsylvania Dutch country. Their cookery is enjoyed and copied.

The German people first came into old Lancaster County. As they spread out they placed their stamp on Berks, Northumberland, Lebanon, Northampton, Lehigh, and Montgomery counties. Lancaster, Bethlehem, Allentown, Kutztown, Lebanon, and Norristown are principal centers. Highway 30 runs through the heart of the region, and there are smaller centers in other parts of the state. The annual Pennsylvania Dutch Folk Festival at Kutztown near Reading attracts 100,000 people.

HARRISBURG

Many authorities have called the Pennsylvania capitol at Harrisburg "the finest capitol building in the nation." Covering 2 acres (.81 hectare), with 649 rooms, it is dominated by a dome resembling that of St. Peter's in Rome. Lifting a garlanded mace at the top is a statue representing the commonwealth. The building, designed by Joseph M. Houston, was finished in 1906. The North and South office buildings, Education Building, and Finance Building are other fine state structures.

The magnificent William Penn Memorial Museum and Archives Building provides a proper setting for the treasures of the capital. The mammoth statue of William Penn, by Pennsylvania's sculptor Janet de Coux, pays tribute to the leader whose name the museum bears. Here is the precious original Penn charter for Pennsylvania. The great Gettysburg paintings by Rothermel now have a permanent home here. One of these is the largest battle scene in North America on a single canvas. The five-story circular structure houses exhibits of Indian life, collections of transportation equipment, natural history exhibits, and many others that bring alive the story of Pennsylvania's rich heritage.

John Harris Mansion, home of the city's founder, is now headquarters of the Dauphin County Historical Society. The Pennsylvania State Farm Show is the largest indoor free agricultural show in the world and is probably the only farm show held in January. It accommodates thirteen acres (five hectares) of displays under one roof. The capital is also noted for its annual Pennsylvania National Horse Show, Standard Bred Horse Sale, and Pennsylvania Livestock Show.

TOWARD THE WEST

State College is home of the enormous Pennsylvania State University, Pennsylvania's land grant institution. Its college of mineral industries is one of the most notable of its kind in the world.

Near State College is the shrine of the famed Pennsylvania 28th Division. Bellefonte was the home of five governors of Pennsylvania. It received its name when noted French visitor Talleyrand exclaimed "What a beautiful fountain!" when he saw the large spring there.

Ole Bull State Park in Porter County preserves the memories of an unusual colony in Pennsylvania. Bull, the spirited Norwegian violinist, dreamed of a home in America where Norwegians of talent could bring their abilities to full flower. He invested in a development of land on Kettle Creek. In 1852, when he unfurled a banner bearing the name Oleana, the Norwegians who had arrived gave thirty-one cheers, one for each state in the union and three for their leader. New Norway was dedicated that day.

Unfortunately, the project did not succeed, and Bull lost both his dreams of a haven and a great deal of money. Legend says that when the blow came he wandered into the woods playing his violin. Then half-crazed with grief, he shattered his violin and buried the pieces in the mountains.

Drake Well Memorial Park near Titusville pays tribute to the man and the oil industry which he founded. Also in the park is a museum of the petroleum industry.

One of America's prize relics is the restored hull of Oliver Hazard Perry's flagship *Niagara,* displayed at Erie. A monument to Perry stands between Presque Isle and Misty Bay. Another Perry site is the Perry Memorial House and Dickson Tavern at Erie. Presque Isle is one of the nation's most unusual state parks, located on a seven-mile (eleven-kilometer) finger of land thrusting into Lake Erie. The Erie region is one of the great freshwater "sea" resorts. The prow of the U.S. *Wolverine,* first iron ship of the navy, is preserved as a memorial at Erie, near the *Niagara.* The Erie Public Museum and Planetarium presents interesting displays on the Battle of Lake Erie.

At Waterford, south of Erie, Fort Le Boeuf Museum contains an interesting collection of frontier artifacts. A monument commemorates the visit of young George Washington to the fort.

Opposite: Oliver Hazard Perry's restored flagship Niagara, *at Erie.*

George Washington is remembered in western as well as eastern Pennsylvania. A seventy-foot (twenty-one-meter) cross marks the spot near Waterford where he delivered the message to Fort Le Boeuf that triggered the French and Indian War. Fort Necessity, where Washington surrendered in that same war, has been restored at Farmington by the National Park Service. The town of Washington provides further recognition for the man who began his public career in the region and later became the Father of His Country.

Another restoration is that of Fort Ligonier at Ligonier. It offers one of the world's finest collections of equipment and momentos from the French and Indian War.

An attraction of a different type is the renowned home called Falling Waters, designed by architect Frank Lloyd Wright. This showplace is owned by the Western Pennsylvania Conservatory and is now open to the public on request.

Two unusual events enliven the area. Stahlstown holds its annual Flax Scutching Festival, and a Maple Sugar Festival is held each year near Meyersdale in Somerset County.

At Grandview Cemetery in Johnstown is a blank headstone, marking the graves of 777 unidentified victims of the great flood there. Conemaugh Gap at the west end of the city is a picturesque gorge 1,700 feet (518 meters) deep and 7 miles (11 kilometers) long.

Bushy Run Battlefield is where Colonel Henry Bouquet's decisive victory over the Indians took place. In 1918, school children of Westmoreland County donated their pennies to make possible the purchase of 6½ acres (2.63 hectares) of the battlefield site. The Bushy Run area is now a state park.

The region of Aliquippa and Ambridge was the scene of some of the most unusual experimental settlements in the country. A religious leader, George Rapp, who persuaded his followers to donate all their property to his Harmony Society, built a colony where all would await the second coming of Christ. Their first colony was called Harmony, north of present Aliquippa. In addition to the spiritual emphasis, they prospered.

Suddenly Rapp sold the colony and all moved to New Harmony in Indiana. They were successful there; then just as suddenly they sold

84

New Harmony and returned to Pennsylvania, setting up the colony of Economy, at present Ambridge. Their factories produced textiles of high quality, their farms were productive, and they invested in many enterprises. Gradually, however, the colony declined and was dissolved in 1905. Seventeen buildings, all restored, are now preserved to give visitors an idea of the life of this unusual community.

MAGNIFICENT REVIVAL

At the end of World War II, Mayor David Lawrence called his city, Pittsburgh, the "dirtiest slag pile in the United States." When architect Frank Lloyd Wright was asked for his proposals, he said, "Abandon it!" Someone remarked that if the pall of smoke ever lifted, there probably would be nothing there at all.

With one of the finest examples of the cooperation of all groups and all the people, the smog has been greatly reduced, and a great new city has emerged.

Where the Allegheny and Monongahela join, Point State Park is now a spot of beauty. All that remains of old Fort Pitt, the famed blockhouse, may still be seen in Point State Park. Adjacent to this park is Gateway Center, a twenty-three acre (nine-hectare) improvement with stainless steel skyscrapers, a vast hotel, and a two-acre (nearly one-hectare) garden with underground garage. The Alcoa Building has been called "one of the country's most daring experiments in skyscraper design." It was built from the inside, completely without scaffolding.

Mellon Square is a formal garden of trees, lawns, flowers, and sparkling fountains. Beneath it is a five-level parking garage. The Civic Arena was built at the base of the Golden Triangle. This was the world's first "convertible" sports arena, with a retractable dome that can be opened in good weather. The city's new look has cost nearly three billion dollars so far.

Only one steel mill remains in Pittsburgh proper, but the city's industrial might has not declined. Almost 20 percent of the nation's steel capacity is still found in metropolitan Pittsburgh. Since World War II, scores of new manufacturing companies have opened there. As "Gateway to the West," the city   one of the greatest inland river ports, handling millions of tons a year.

The dynamic transformation of Pittsburgh, and the vital re-creation of Philadelphia, call for tribute to the spirit of Pennsylvanians. Not content to rest on the mighty achievements of the past, they press forward to retain leadership in a new era.

Pittsburgh's Golden Triangle, where the Monongahela and Allegheny rivers join.

Handy Reference Section

Instant Facts

Official name—Commonwealth of Pennsylvania
Became second state, December 12, 1787
Capital—Harrisburg
Nickname—The Keystone State
State motto—Virtue, Liberty and Independence
State animal—Whitetail deer
State dog—Great Dane
State bird—Ruffed grouse
State fish—Brook trout
State flower—Mountain laurel
State tree—Eastern hemlock
Area—45,333 square miles (117,412 square kilometers)
Rank in area—33rd
Shoreline—89 miles (143 kilometers)
Greatest length (north to south)—176 miles (283 kilometers)
Greatest width (east to west)—302 miles (486 kilometers)
Geographic center—2½ miles (4 kilometers) southwest of Bellefonte
Highest point—3,213 feet (979 meters), Mount Davis
Lowest point—sea level
Number of counties—67
Population—1980 census: 11,879,679 (1993 estimate: 12,136,900)
Rank in population—4th
Population density—262 per square mile (101 per square kilometer), 1980 census
Rank in density—8th
Population Center—In Centre Township, Perry County, .8 mile (1.29
　　　　　　　kilometers) north of Bloomfield

Major Cities	1980 Census	1990 Estimate
Philadelphia	1,684,740	1,557,637
Pittsburgh	423,959	400,681
Erie	119,123	111,713
Allentown	103,758	102,220
Scranton	88,117	82,299

You Have a Date with History

1608—Captain John Smith may have visited Pennsylvania
1609—Henry Hudson sails lower Delaware River
1615—Etienne Brulé traverses route of Susquehanna River
1643—First permanent settlement (Swedish) established by Johan Printz
1655—Dutch conquer Swedish settlements
1664—English seize territory

1681—Charles II grants land to William Penn
1682—Philadelphia founded; Penn lands in Pennsylvania
1683—First Germans come to Pennsylvania at Germantown
1703—Delaware separates from Pennsylvania
1718—William Penn dies
1723—Benjamin Franklin comes to Philadelphia
1737—"Walking" Purchase
1753—Washington goes to Fort Le Boeuf
1754—French and Indian War begins
1763—Pontiac War
1769—James Smith captures Fort Bedford
1774—First Continental Congress meets at Carpenters Hall, Philadelphia
1775—Second Continental Congress meets at State House, Philadelphia
1776—Declaration of Independence accepted July 4, Independence Hall
1777—Howe enters Philadelphia
1778—Franklin brings about alliance with France
1787—Constitutional Convention meets at Independence Hall; Pennsylvania
        becomes second state on December 12
1790—Philadelphia becomes United States capital
1799—Lancaster is capital of Pennsylvania
1812—Capital of Pennsylvania moved to Harrisburg; war comes
1813—Perry's fleet built at Erie
1827—Mechanics Union of Trade Associations formed at Philadelphia
1838—New Pennsylvania Constitution approved
1859—First petroleum well in history spouts at Titusville
1862—First invasion of Pennsylvania in Civil War
1863—Battle of Gettysburg
1873—Present Constitution of Pennsylvania adopted
1876—Centennial Exposition held at Philadelphia
1881—American Federation of Labor organized at Pittsburgh
1889—Flood disaster at Johnstown
1918—28th Division helps stem Germans at the Marne
1919—660,000 Pennsylvanians had served in World World I
1920—World's first commercial broadcasting station at Pittsburgh
1926—Sesqui-Centennial Exposition at Philadelphia
1944—300th anniversary of first permanent Pennsylvania settlement
1946—1,200,000 Pennsylvanians had served in World War II
1950—400,000 Pennsylvanians in uniform in Korean War
1957—Boy Scout jamboree at Valley Forge
1965—William Penn Memorial Museum and Archives Building dedicated
1967—First Constitutional Convention in 94 years is held
1971—Giant electric power complex is completed
1971—State operated lottery is established
1972—Hurricane Agnes causes worst storm damage
1975—Population drops to third in nation
1976—"Legionnaires' Disease" strikes
1979—Accident at Three Mile nuclear power plant created threat of a high-level
        radiation discharge

1985—Reconstruction of area bombed by police to drive out rebel group MOVE in Philadelphia; multiple tornadoes rampage in northwestern Pennsylvania leaving 56 dead, 200 injured, and enormous property damage
1987—Doctors at Pittsburgh Children's Hospital successfully transplant five organs into 3-year-old Tabatha Foster
1990—Flash floods inundate wide areas of Western Pennsylvania destroying crop lands and homes

Governors (since statehood)

Benjamin Franklin 1785-1788
Thomas Mifflin 1788-1799
Thomas McKean 1799-1808
Simon Snyder 1808-1817
William Findlay 1817-1820
Joseph Hiester 1820-1823
John Andrew Shulze, 1823-1829
George Wolf 1829-1835
Joseph Ritner 1835-1839
David Rittenhouse Porter 1839-1845
Francis Rawn Shunk 1845-1848
William Freame Johnston 1848-1852
William Bigler 1852-1855
James Pollock 1855-1858
William Fisher Packer 1858-1861
Andrew Gregg Curtin 1861-1867
John White Geary 1867-1873
John Frederick Hartranft 1873-1879
Henry Martyn Hoyt 1879-1883
Robert Emory Pattison 1883-1887
James Addams Beaver 1887-1891
Robert Emory Pattison 1891-1895
Daniel Hartman Hastings 1895-1899

William Alexis Stone 1899-1903
Samuel Whitaker Pennypacker 1903-1907
Edwin Sydney Stuart 1907-1911
John Kinley Tener 1911-1915
Martin Grove Brumbaugh 1915-1919
William Cameron Sproul 1919-1923
Gifford Pinchot 1923-1927
John Stuchell Fisher 1927-1931
Gifford Pinchot 1931-1935
George Howard Earle 1935-1939
Arthur Horace James 1939-1943
Edward Martin 1943-1947
John C. Bell 1947-1947
James H. Duff 1947-1951
John S. Fine 1951-1955
George M. Leader 1955-1959
David L. Lawrence 1959-1963
William W. Scranton 1963-1967
Raymond P. Shafer 1967-1971
Milton J. Shapp 1971-1979
Richard L. Thornburgh 1979-1987
Robert P. Casey 1987-

Thinkers, Doers, Fighters

People of renown who have been associated with Pennsylvania

Allen, Richard
Anderson, Marian
Arnold, H.H. (Hap)
Baldwin, Matthias
Barber, Samuel
Barry, John
Benet, Stephen Vincent
Bouquet, Henry
Brown, Charles Brockden
Buchanan, James

Burleigh, Henry T.
Cadman, Charles Wakefield
Calder, Alexander
Cameron, Simon
Carnegie, Andrew
Cornplanter (Chief)
Curtin, Andrew G.
Decatur, Stephen
Dobbins, Daniel
Drake, Edwin L.

Drawbaugh, Daniel
Eichholtz, Jacob
Eisenhower, Dwight David
Forbes, John
Ford, John B.
Foster, Stephen Collins
Franklin, Benjamin
Frick, Henry Clay
Gallatin, Albert
Girard, Stephen
Hays, Isaac
Heinz, Henry J.
Herbert, Victor
Hershey, Milton S.
Huntingdon, Joseph Saxton
Kelly, Grace
Logan, James (Chief)
Marshall, George Catlett
Mathewson, Christopher (Christy)
McClellan, George B.
Meade, George
Mellon, Andrew
Mennin, Peter
Morley, Christopher
Morris, Gouverneur
Morris, Robert

Nevin, Ethelbert
Parrish, Maxfield
Peary, Robert E.
Penn, Hannah
Penn, William
Physick, Philip Syng
Pinchot, Gifford
Porter, David D.
Priestley, Joseph
Rapp, George
Rinehart, Mary Roberts
Rothermel, Peter Frederick
St. Clair, Arthur
Shikellamy (Chief)
Stanton, Edwin M.
Tarbell, Ida M.
Wanamaker, John
Washington, George
Wayne, Anthony (''Mad'')
West, Benjamin
Westinghouse, George
Wiggin, Kate Douglas
Wilmot, David
Wilson, James
Woolworth, F.W.
Zenger, Peter

The cast house (furnace) at the Hopewell Village ironmaking community.

Index

94

Hopewell Village National Historic Site

PICTURE CREDITS

ABOUT THE AUTHOR

With the publication of his first book for school use when he was twenty, **Allan Carpenter** began a career as an author that has spanned more than 135 books. After teaching in the public schools of Des Moines, Mr. Carpenter began his career as an educational publisher at the age of twenty-one when he founded the magazine *Teachers Digest*. In the field of educational periodicals, he was responsible for many innovations. During his many years in publishing, he has perfected a highly organized approach to handling large volumes of factual material: after extensive traveling and having collected all possible materials, he systematically reviews and organizes everything. From his apartment high in Chicago's John Hancock Building, Allan recalls, "My collection and assimilation of materials on the states and countries began before the publication of my first book." Allan is the founder of Carpenter Publishing House and of Infordata International, Inc., publishers of *Issues in Education* and *Index to U. S. Government Periodicals*. When he is not writing or traveling, his principal avocation is music. He has been the principal bassist of many symphonies, and he managed the country's leading non-professional symphony for twenty-five years.

96